AMERICAN
HERITAGE

December 1957 · Volume IX, Number 1

"THE LONG SPEECH"

George Catlin, famous painter of the American Indians, knew his
subjects intimately. He understood not only their stoicism and courage
but also the humorous aspects of their lives. Among the more than
1,200 paintings in which, between 1830 and 1870, he recorded their
"looks and customs" is this lampoon of their unconscionably long-winded
powwows. A pompous chief still gestures and declaims, and though
one brave manages to keep the calumet going, barely the scalp
locks of the rest of his audience show above the drifting snow.

AMERICAN HERITAGE

The Magazine of History

PUBLISHER
James Parton

EDITORIAL DIRECTOR
Joseph J. Thorndike, Jr.

EDITOR
Bruce Catton

MANAGING EDITOR
Oliver Jensen

ASSOCIATE EDITOR
Richard M. Ketchum

ASSISTANT EDITOR
Joan Paterson Mills

EDITORIAL ASSISTANTS
Hilde Heun, Stephen W. Sears
Caroline Backlund, Lilyan Goldman
Art: Murray Belsky, Trudy Glucksberg

ART DIRECTOR
Irwin Glusker

ADVISORY BOARD
Allan Nevins, *Chairman*

Carl Carmer   Richard P. McCormick
Albert B. Corey   Harry Shaw Newman
Christopher Crittenden Howard H. Peckham
Marshall Davidson   S. K. Stevens
Louis C. Jones   Arthur M. Schlesinger, Sr.

REGIONAL EDITORS
Ray A. Billington..........*Evanston, Illinois*
John W. Caughey.....*Los Angeles, California*
K. Ross Toole.............*Helena, Montana*
Walter Prescott Webb.........*Austin, Texas*

STAFF PHOTOGRAPHER
Herbert Loebel

CIRCULATION DIRECTOR
Richard V. Benson

AMERICAN HERITAGE is published every two months by American Heritage Publishing Co., Inc., 551 Fifth Avenue, New York 17, N. Y.

Single Copies: $2.95

Annual Subscriptions: $12.50 in the U.S.A.
$13.50 elsewhere

An annual Index of AMERICAN HERITAGE is published every February, priced at $1.00. AMERICAN HERITAGE is also indexed in *Readers' Guide to Periodical Literature.*

AMERICAN HERITAGE will consider but assumes no responsibility for unsolicited material. All such submissions should be accompanied by a stamped, self-addressed envelope.

Sponsored by

American Association for State & Local History · Society of American Historians

CONTENTS   *December, 1957 · Volume IX, Number 1*

COVERS: A century ago, before the steam locomotive shed its bright colors, builders like Seth Wilmarth signaled each new achievement with fine lithographs of their work. We are indebted to The Old Print Shop in New York for the one on the front cover, depicting Wilmarth's *Troy* of 1856, a classic "American" type engine, the kind that dominated nineteenth-century railroading. On the back cover is *The Belle of the Winter,* all done up in ermine tippet, muff, and trim—not to mention overskirt, underskirt, and Heaven knows what else. This rare Currier & Ives print from the Harry T. Peters Collection appears by courtesy of the Museum of the City of New York.

Eliot at 55, in a formal portrait painted from life by an unknown artist in 1659.

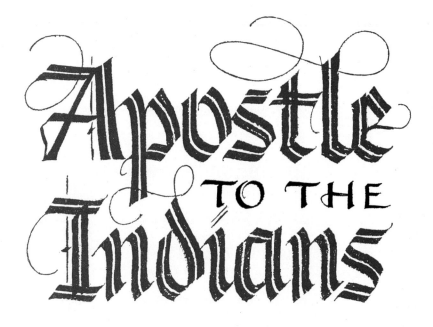

Apostle TO THE Indians

John Eliot preached to the Massachusetts savages, printed the Bible in their "barbarous Linguo," and tried to reply to their disquieting questions

By FRANCIS RUSSELL

Whenever the Reverend John Eliot walked along the Indian trail from Roxbury to Dorchester Mill in the autumn weather, he tried to put the time to proper use by continuing the metrical version of the Psalms that he and Richard Mather and Thomas Weld were working on. His somber figure pinpointed the brightness of the afternoon as he strode along, heedless of the crickets' antiphonal shrilling. Late goldenrod and Michaelmas daisies encroached on the way, brushing against his cloak. Slowly, so very slowly, the Old Testament lines formed themselves in his mind:

Like Pelican in wilderness
like Owle in desart so am I;
I watch, and like a sparrow am
on house top solitarily.
Mine enemies daily mee reproach . . .

But then, as had happened so many times before, he would find himself caught up in the immediacy of the sun-drenched moment, the shout of the crickets drowning out the psalm. And he would become aware again of sweet fern and the salt scent of the marsh and the harbor in the middle distance and the russet patches of oak and blueberry. Lemon-pale witch hazel fila-

ments, that New World shrub that flowered so strangely in the autumn, came just on a level with his eye. *Nova Anglia*—New England. This, he now knew with loving thankfulness, was his world.

According to the 1628 charter of Massachusetts Bay the "royall intention and the adventurer's free profession, the principall ende of this Plantation" was "to wynn the natives of the country to the knowledge and obedience of the onlie true God and Saviour of mankinde." It was not a profession which many of the earlier settlers shared. Fortunately for them, the Indians of the region had been almost exterminated by a plague a few years before, and there was little challenge in the broken remnants of the Massachusetts Bay tribes. For those transplanted Englishmen the Indians were a subhuman nuisance, when they were not devils. "The veriest Ruines of Mankind," Cotton Mather said of them. And even the gentle Roger Williams called them "wolves with the brains of men."

John Eliot was one of the very few to take the intentions of the charter to heart. Holding the Bible as the literal word of God, the ultimate source of all knowledge, he was drawn to the Indians at least in part by his belief that they were the descendants of

5

the lost tribes of Israel. But more fundamentally they were to him human beings created by God, souls to be saved. This conviction expanded in his inner self until it dominated his life. As he wrote in later years: "Pity to the poor Indians, and desire to make the name of Christ chief in these dark ends of the earth —and not the rewards of men—were the very first and chief moves, if I know what did first and chiefly move in my heart, when God was pleased to put upon me that work of preaching to them."

John Eliot, known to after generations as the Apostle to the Indians, was born at Widford, Hertfordshire, in 1604. At the customary age of fourteen he entered Jesus College, Cambridge, taking his B.A. degree in 1622. He then became an usher in the Reverend Thomas Hooker's school at Little Baddow, an employment that Cotton Mather in later years tried anxiously to show as not really menial. Hooker, a Puritan of the milder sort and much honored in the countryside, was finally forced by Laud's high church policies to flee to Holland as the first step on his way to America. Eliot followed him.

Though John Eliot never wavered from the ferocious creed of Calvin, he kept beneath all the doctrines of predestination a warm and loving heart. Children and Indians he cherished with much patience. There was no Barebones self-righteousness about him. When he left England, a "select number of his pious and Christian friends" followed him on the promise that he would be their New World pastor—an indication of this unordained young man's winning ways. On his arrival he was probably the first New England minister to take orders in the Congregational manner. A year later his bride-to-be, Anne Mumford, came to join him.

At first, he filled in as a substitute in Boston's First Church, and although the elders would have kept him, he was mindful of his friends. There, in the hilly country beyond Boston Neck with its outcroppings of conglomerate and the broken glimpses of the harbor islands, he and his congregation that had followed him so far made their settlement. So was the church in Roxbury established in 1632, and there Eliot remained through wars and changes of governments and dynasties for over fifty years.

In 1646 the General Court of Massachusetts passed an order to promote the diffusion of Christianity among the natives, and the elders of the churches were requested to consider how it might best be effected. Although John Eliot had spent a dozen years tending the rude and straggling Roxbury settlement, he had long been considering just this. He now took into his house Cockenöe, an Indian made prisoner in the Pequot War of 1637, who had been serviced to a Dorchester planter, and who could speak and even read English. Later, an Indian youth named Job Nesutan replaced Cockenöe as Eliot's teacher and helper. With him Eliot began his study of the Indian language, tentatively translating the Commandments and the Lord's Prayer. After two years he was able to preach, if haltingly, in this acquired tongue.

The language of the Massachusetts Bay tribes was Algonquian, a Mahican dialect called by Eliot and others the "Massachusetts language." With the Indian method of compressing complex ideas into extended

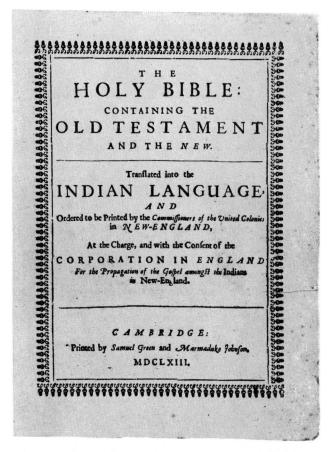

These are the English and (opposite page) *the Indian title pages of Eliot's Algonquian Bible. Financed by a London missionary society, it was the first Bible printed in America.*

single words, it was not a facile tool. Eliot did his best to develop grammatical usages. Cotton Mather held that it would have been more effective to teach the Indians English than to translate Scriptures into their "barbarous Linguo." Even the demons of Hell could not understand it, he said. Gravely Mather explained that he had tried out some languages on a captive audience of demons (whom he reached through conversing with a "possessed" young woman); during the séance, he went on, his infernal friends did well enough with Latin, Greek, and Hebrew, but failed miserably to understand his questions in Algonquian.

Eliot's first mission, when he felt he had mastered the language sufficiently, was at the small Indian settlement near the falls of the Charles River a few miles above Cambridge. Here, on a hill beyond the river's great S curve, Waban—in Algonquian, "the Wind"—a peaceful Indian, half trader, half sachem, had gathered together a settlement out of the fragmented tribes. Waban's group had been friendly to the English from the beginning, and Waban would gladly listen to the stocky man in black who spoke,

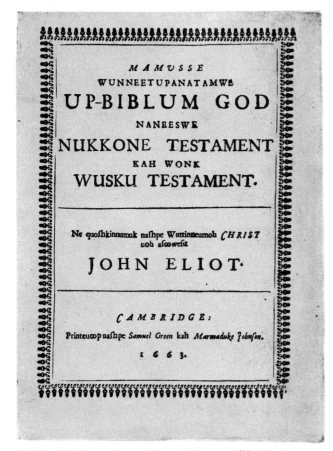

As the title page shows, Algonquian was, like German, agglutinative. The Bible's longest word (34 letters) is Wutappesittukqussunnookwehtunkquoh—"kneeling down to him."

or seemed to speak, the Indian tongue.

It was a fading October day with the hard-rimmed sky beginning to take on tones of winter, when Eliot and three clergymen companions first arrived before Waban's wigwam. There at the council fire Eliot preached the first Protestant sermon in the Indian tongue on the North American continent. He took as his text Ezekiel 27:9, "Prophesy unto the wind, prophesy, son of man, and say to the wind, Thus saith the Lord God." It was a shrewd and happy choice, appealing both to the pride of Waban the Wind and to the superstition of his listeners. Snake eyes reflected by the firelight, elders with bronze impassive faces, the restless children, the shrill-voiced crones silent for once, all watched the Englishman. He preached to them for an hour and a quarter, moderate by that day's standard, adapting as he could the Institutes of Calvin to their forest ways.

After prayers in English—for he did not as yet feel himself equal to praying in Algonquian—some of the Indians began to ask him questions, and he encouraged them then and for all future meetings.

Why, they would ask him around their smoldering fires and later in the lodges of the praying towns, why does not God who has full power kill the Devil that makes all men so bad? Was the Devil or man made first? Might there be something, if only a little, gained by praying to the Devil? If God made Hell in one of the six days, why did he make it before Adam had sinned? If all the world be burned up, where shall Hell be then? Are all the Indians who have died now in Hell, while only we are in the way of getting to Heaven? Why does not God give all men good hearts that they may be good? Whither do dying little children go, seeing they have not sinned? "This question," said Eliot, "gave occasion to teach them more fully original sin and the damned state of all men. I could give them no further comfort than that, when God elects the parents, he elects their seed also."

There were also the curious, the doubting, and the malicious. How is it that sea water is salt and land water fresh? they asked the white man facing them with the clasped book. Or—If a man should be enclosed in iron a foot thick, and thrown into a fire, how would his soul get out? Why do Englishmen kill all snakes?

Waban, however he understood predestination, became a convert to Eliot's teaching. Under his leadership and with Eliot's instructions, the Indians of his settlement formed themselves into the Christian village of Nonantum—meaning "Rejoicing"—after the white man's pattern. From Eliot they received clothing, blankets, spades, axes, and other tools. The squaws were given spinning wheels. For out of these nomad hunters he would make husbandmen, that they should eat bread in the sweat of their dark faces. The Indians laid out streets and fenced and planted their fields. Eliot was understanding, and they trusted him. He knew he could not push the mercurial savages too hard, and he was content at first if they observed the decent minimum of outer forms. One group of Indians, instructed not to do any unnecessary work on Sunday, replied that it would be easy for them since they had little to do on any day.

Nonantum developed into a small trading center

where the Indians made brooms, baskets, and eelpots for the colonists and sold fish and venison and berries in season. Yet the Praying Indians, as they were called, were looked on with contemptuous distrust by most whites, and finally Eliot resolved to move them up the Charles River to a remote place of hills called Natick, eighteen miles away. On this virgin ground he would set up a town according to the principles laid down in the Bible. Eliot would have his Indians "wholly governed by Scriptures in all things, both in church and state."

Natick was laid out for some 800 inhabitants. Except for the temporary assistance of an English carpenter, all the work was done by Indians. Two streets on one side of the river were joined to one on the far side by a bridge. After the lots were measured they were assigned one to a family. A circular fort was built and after that a rectangular meetinghouse fifty feet long, twenty-five feet wide, and twelve feet high. The latter was used as a schoolroom during the week, one section of it being partitioned off for Eliot's particular use and known as the Prophet's Chamber. There were several other houses of the English kind, but for the most part the Indians preferred their accustomed wigwams.

nce every fortnight, during the summer weather, Eliot visited his Praying Indians at Natick. Summoned by two drums, the congregation assembled in the meetinghouse. There, in the church he had helped build with his own hands, in the smoky, rush-lit room with the noise of running water outside and inside the high-pitched buzz of mosquitoes, Eliot would deliver one of those massive seventeenth-century sermons, expounding the Scriptures in the tongue he had learned with so much difficulty. The Indians had come to regard him as a father. Beyond the dogma which they scarcely understood they sensed the goodness of the man. So they served him, with only occasional backsliding, and when the times of trouble came most of them held loyally to him.

Natick became a show place, visited frequently by Boston clergymen who were pleased to catechize the congregation through an interpreter and delighted at the answers that were roared back. Men like Governor Endicott and President Dunster of Harvard, who came to Natick and saw the domesticated Indians hoeing, reaping, picking hops, cutting wood, making hay, and building stone fences, were happily convinced. The harder minds among the colonists were not. Most of the settlers looked sourly on Eliot's Indians, maintaining that their piety was a fable, a device for raising money to support a group of hypocritical and shiftless "foreigners."

Although Eliot's biographers do not emphasize the fact, there were tangible advantages in becoming a Praying Indian. The apostle wanted his converts to be prosperous as a mark of election, and he had the means to reward those who listened to the Gospel message. Clothing, food, and implements were on hand for them. Never did he enter a settlement without bringing gifts, for children as well as the others. No Indian was ever turned away empty-handed from the door of the Roxbury parsonage. It has been estimated that the cost of conversion ran to £10 per Indian, a large sum in those days.

Eliot, selfless and austere, had been known to give away his monthly stipend in a fit of absent-minded benevolence; but like many such unworldly men he could be singularly practical in raising money for a cause. The funds for his missionary work came from England, through the middle-aged piety of dowagers of wealthy Puritan families and occasional aristocrats like the daughter of the Earl of Shrewsbury. Eliot planned his touches with care. He was the earliest and one of the most successful writers of dunning letters in America, the first transatlantic promoter of a fund-raising campaign. In 1649 a London corporation, the Society for Promoting and Propagating the Gospel of Jesus Christ in New England, was established, and on this society Eliot came to depend for much of his later support, including the subsidizing of his Bible translation.

The question of the sincerity of the Indian converts is a complex one. How much they were swayed by religious conviction is impossible to say. Certainly the awe and admiration they felt for the dominant white men was easily transferable to the white men's peculiar God. Then, too, in their eroded tribal state they were driven to the shelter of the white settlements by fear of the Mohawks. By becoming converts they freed themselves of the oppressive exactions of sachem and medicine man. There were the things of this world—not to be neglected—that were to be had in Christ's name. Finally there was the influence of the Reverend John Eliot himself, the doughty, paternal figure whose kindliness even Calvin's creed could not conceal.

Eliot's translation of the Bible into Algonquian, *Mamusse Wunneetupanatamwe Up-Biblum God* ("The-whole Holy his-Bible God"), was his most cherished achievement, the goal of all his studies. From his first days in New England he had seen it as his sacred task to bring the word of God to the Indians. Only when they could read the Bible could he be assured of the permanence of their faith.

Wutontſeongaſh Chriſt **Chap. 1.** *wunneetuonk Jeſus Chriſt*

WUNAUNCHEMOOKAONK NASHPE
MATTHEVV.

CHAP. I.

a Luke 3.23.
b Gen. 21.3.
c Gen. 25. 26.
d Gen. 29. 35.
e Gen. 38. 27.
f 1 Chr. 2.5.
Ruth 4.18.

Ppometuongane *a* book Jeſus Chriſt, wunnaumonuh David, wunnaumonuh Abraham.

2 *b* Abraham wunnaumonieu Iſaakoh, kah *c* Iſaak wunnaumonieu Jakobuh, kah *d* Jakob wunnaumonieu Judaſoh, kah weematoh.

3 Kah *e* Judas wunnaumonieu Phareſoh kah Zarahoh wutch Tamarhut, kah *f* Phares wunnaumonieu Ezromoh, kah Ezrom wunnaumonieu Aramoh.

4 Kah Aram wunnaumonieu Aminadaboh, kah Aminadab wunnaumonieu Naaſſonoh, kah Naaſſon wunnaumonieu Salmonoh.

5 Kah Salmon wunnaumonieu Boazoh wutch Rachab, kah Boaz wunnaumonieu Obeduh wutch Ruth, kah Obed wunnaumonieu Jeſſeuh.

g 1 Sam. 16.1. & 17.12.

6 Kah *g* Jeſſe wunnaumonieu David ketaſſootoh, kah *h* David ketaſſoot wunnaumonieu Solomonoh wutch ummittamwuſſuh Uriah.

h 2 Sam. 12. 24.
i 1 Chr. 3. 10.

7 Kah *i* Solomon wunnaumonieu Rehoboamoh, kah Rehoboam wunnaumonieu Abiahoh, kah Abia wunnaumonieu Aſahoh.

8 Kah Aſa wunnaumonieu Joſaphatoh, kah Joſaphat wunnaumonieu Joramoh, kah Joram wnnnaumonieu Oziaſoh.

9 Kah Ozias wunnaumonieu Jothamoh, kah Jotham wunnaumonieu Achazoh, kah Achaz wunnaumonieu Ezekiaſoh.

k 2 Kin. 20. 21.
1 Chro. 3. 10.

10 Kah *k* Ezekias wunnaumonieu Manaſſes, kah Manaſſes wunnaumonieu Ammonoh, kah Ammon wunnaumonieu Joſiaſoh.

11 Kah Joſias wunnaumonieu Jechoniaſoh, kah wematoh, ut papaume na uttooche máſinneohteámuk ut Babylon.

l 1 Chr. 3. 16, 17.

12 Kah mahche miſſinneohteábettit ut Babylon, *l* Jechonias wunnaumonieu Saláthieloh, kah Salathiel wunnaumonieu Zorobabeloh.

13 Kah Zorobabel wunnaumonieu Abiudoh, kah Abiud wunnaumonieu Eliakimoh, kah Eliakim wunnaumonieu Azoroh.

14 Kah Azor wunnaumonieu Sadokoh, kah Sadok wunnaumonieu Achimoh, kah Achim wunnaumonieu Eliudoh.

15 Kah Eliud wunnaumonieu Eleazaroh, kah Eleazar wunnaumonieu Matthanoh, kah Matthan wunnaumonieu Jakoboh.

16 Kah Jakob wunnaumonieu Joſephoh, weſſukeh Mary noh mo wachegit Jeſus uttiyeuoh áhennit Chriſt.

17 Nemehkuh wame pometeongaſh wutch Abrahamut onk yean Davidut, nabo yauwudt pometeongaſh; neit wutch Davidut onk yean unmiſſinohkonauh ut Babylon, nabo yauwudt pometeongaſh : neit wutch ummiſſinohkonaoh ut Babylon nô pajeh uppeyonat Jeſus Chriſt, nabo yauwudt pometeongaſh.

m Luke 1. 27.

18 Kah Jeſus Chriſt *m* wunneetuonk yeu mo, nagum okaſoh Maryhoh kah Joſeph quoſhodhettit (aſquam naneeſinhettiekup) miſkauau wutchéketeauónat naſhpe Nathauanittooh.

19 Neit weſſukeh Joſephuh wunnomwaénuooh, matta mo wuttenantamooun wutáyimáuoh muſſiſſewautut, unnantam kemeu nuppogken yeuoh.

20 Webe uttwontog yeuſhog kuſſeh wutangelſumoh Lord wunneeihtunkquoh ut unnukquomutonganit, noowau, Joſeph ken wunnaumonuh David, ahque wabeſiſh nemunon Mary kummittamwos, newutche uttiyeuoh wachegit, ne naſhpe wunneetupanatamwe Nathauanittoour.

n Luke 1. 31.

21 Kah woh neechau wuſiaumon woh kuttiſſowen *n* Jeſus, newutche woh wadchanau *n* unmiſſinninnumoh wutch ummatcheſeonga noóout.

22 Wame yeuſh n nihyeupaſh ne woh n niſh tok ancowop Lord naſhpeu manittoowompuh noowau.

o Iſaiah 7. 14.

23 *o* Kuſſeh peenomp piſh wompequau, kah piſh neechau wannaumonuh, kah piſh wuttiſſowenuh Emanuel, yeu nauwuttamun, God koowetomukqun.

24 Neit Joſeph omohket wutch kouénat, wutuſſen uttoh ánukqut wutangelſumoh Lord, kah neemunau ummittamwuſſoh.

25 Kah matta oowabeuh nô pajeh wunneechanat mohtommeginitcheh wunnaumonuh, kah wuttiſſowenuh Jeſus.

CHAP. II.

a Luke 2. 6.

IESUS *a* neekit ut Bethlem ut Judea ukkeſukkodtumut Herod Sontim, kuſſeh waantamwáenuog wamohettit wutchepwoeiyeu Jeruſalemwaut.

A 3   2 Noo-

This is Chapter I of the Gospel according to St. Matthew in Eliot's Indian Bible, recounting the genealogy of Christ. The word wunnaumonieu, *of course, stands for the chapter's ubiquitous "begat."*

Job Nesutan often did not know. And some Indians with childish malice would deliberately trick him, supplying a wrong or sometimes an obscene word.

With his other burdens it is a marvel that he found time to carry on his translating. For in all weathers and all seasons he made his visitations in the towns and friendly settlements, sometimes as far as sixty miles afield. An indomitable figure who could bend to a nor'easter and yet not draw back, who did not hesitate in a pinch to adopt Indian dress, who would stop on a rainy night at any wigwam and wring the water from his socks and be off the next morning, who when hostile Indians barred his path could say: "I fear neither you nor all the sachems in the country. I will go on, and do you touch me if you dare."

Then there was his Roxbury congregation, and the education of his own people. "Lord! For schools everywhere among us!" he prayed. He founded the Indian College at Cambridge. He established the Free School in Roxbury. (Founded in 1645, the Roxbury Latin School, as it was subsequently known, is the oldest endowed school in the United States. It is at present a country day school of 150 students in West Roxbury, Massachusetts.) He made teachers and ministers of his Indian converts. And he wrote reports over the years that were published regularly by the society and came to be known as the Indian Tracts.

For ten years he labored at his self-appointed task, in the long summer evenings, through the waning autumn days, with winter biting at his study door, testing each sentence, each verse. It was a tremendous effort to adapt the restricted Indian tongue to the subtle and majestic cadences of the King James Version. For so many things there were no equivalents.

CONTINUED ON PAGE 117

If Chicago has reason for remembering Valentine's Day, New York has reason, too, for remembering a famous, less grisly fourteenth of February in her own annals. For on that day in 1842 Manhattanites threw sophistication and decorum to the East River winds and put on a public reception that was to be the talk of the town for many a Knickerbocker moon. The occasion was the arrival of a distinguished British visitor, the creator of Pickwick and Little Nell, and the event was the Boz Ball.

Charles Dickens arrived in America just two weeks before his thirtieth birthday. In the six short years since the appearance of the first anonymous number of *The Posthumous Papers of the Pickwick Club*, the young author had made the pen name "Boz" known throughout the world in a record-smashing leap from obscurity to fame. Though he had not yet written the novels most critics rate as his masterpieces, Dickens was already the most widely admired writer of the day. The Yankee excitement over his arrival knew no bounds. Even the idolized Lafayette, during his triumphal tour of America in 1824, had not received a warmer welcome.

Dickens and his wife landed in Boston on January 22, and the Bostonians set about wining and dining the famous novelist with an unprecedented lack of New England reserve. As accounts of events in the city soon popularly referred to as "Boz-town" reached them, envious New Yorkers determined to do something bigger and better than anything done by their rival to the north. A Philadelphia editor, noting the spread of the Boz mania, observed with unbrotherly sarcasm, "The Gothamites outnumber Bostonites and outdollar them and will surely outshine them." And they did.

A formal committee was formed, whose members debated what was to be done in a long series of meetings which grew in heat and violence. A committee in Boston, after similar wrangling, had decided to make their official function a public dinner for men only, so that the occasion could be celebrated with the proper spirits. James Russell Lowell, representing a group with temperance principles, wrote a friend, "I proposed to have a dinner at which women should take the place of wine, and it was voted down by a very large majority." Taking a cue from Lowell, certain members of the New York committee urged that it would be an insult to Mrs. Dickens as well as to the originator of Little Nell to exclude women from any proposed function and suggested giving a grand ball. Philip Hone, the former mayor of New York and one of the committee, recorded in his diary that finally, after a bitter battle between the "dinnerites" and the "ballites," the ballites won, though the dinnerites went ahead with plans for a separate event.

The date for the ball was set for Valentine's Day, and the place finally selected was the Park Theatre. The largest gathering place in New York, the theater had a capacity estimated at 3,000. Tickets were limited to that number and were sold at $5, with a price of $2 for extra ladies (not to exceed two to one party). The 3,000 tickets were subscribed for almost immediately; wealthy New Yorkers were soon offering as high as $40 for them without finding any sellers.

Then the committee began to plan the ball that was to outdo, outshine, and outspend anything of the kind ever given in America. Thousands of dollars were spent on the preparations and decorations. The

The BOZ

TO WELCOME CHARLES DICKENS, NE
AND THEN SPOILED EVERYTHING B

By A

stage was extended to cover the entire theater pit, making a ballroom 150 by 70 feet, with a runway to one of the boxes along which Dickens was to make his grand entrance. Medallion sketches of scenes from Dickens' novels and of the Presidents of the United States were hung on the walls. An American eagle, with a laurel crown in its beak, presided over a huge portrait of Dickens. Elaborate chandeliers, hung by gilded ropes from the high ceiling, and innumerable candelabra made the theater a brilliant show. Flowers, draperies, 7,000 yards of bunting, and flags and insignia of all the states added to the spectacle.

Central attraction of the evening (after Boz himself) was to be the series of *tableaux vivants* pantomiming scenes from the guest of honor's novels. These, presented between dances on a raised platform at one end of the ballroom, included such scenes as "Mrs. Leo Hunter's dress, *déjeuner*," "The Pickwick Club," "The middle-aged lady in the double-bedded room," "Mrs. Bardell faints in Mr. Pickwick's arms," "Mrs. Bardell encounters Mr. Pickwick in prison," "The red-nosed man discourseth," "Mr. and Mrs. Mantalini in Ralph Nickleby's office," "Oliver Twist at Mr. Maylie's door," "Little Nell leading her grandfather," and—as the grand climax to the evening—the representation of "Washington Irving in England and Charles Dickens in America."

Nor were the eyes alone to be feasted. Refreshments were prepared by 140 men and women, who worked three days and three nights, and served by 66 waiters the night of the ball. One of the feminine guests later wrote a friend that the crowd of 3,000 consumed—among other things—50 hams, 50 tongues, 28,000 stewed oysters, 10,000 pickled oysters, 4,000 candy kisses, and 6,000 candy mottoes. "I am afraid at this rate," she added, "oysters will become very scarce." Another report that 5,000 plates, 800 cups and saucers, and 4,000 glasses and tumblers were used gives a hint as to the relative popularity of the champagne, tea, and chocolate served.

The whole affair was brilliantly ordered and managed. Dickens was especially impressed by the police management of the carriage traffic, which extended at times over a quarter of a mile in length; in England, he remarked, the situation would have been completely chaotic. In a letter to his friend and, later, biographer, John Forster, Dickens described the ball:

At a quarter-past 9 exactly, we were waited upon by David Colden Esquire, and General George Morris; habited, the former in full ball costume, the latter in the full dress uniform of Heaven knows what regiment of militia. The general took Kate, Colden gave his arm to me, and we proceeded downstairs to a carriage at the door, which took us to the stage-door of the theatre, greatly to the disappointment of an enormous crowd who were besetting the main door and making a most tremendous hullaballoo. The scene on our entrance was very striking. There were three thousand people present in full dress; from the roof to the floor, the theatre was decorated magnificently; and the light, glitter, glare, show, noise, and cheering, baffle my descriptive powers. We were walked in through the centre of the centre dress-box, the front whereof was taken out for the occasion; so to the back of the stage, where the mayor and other dignitaries received us: and we were then paraded all round the enormous ball-room twice, for the gratification of the many-headed. That done, we began to dance—Heaven knows how we did it, for there was no room. And we continued dancing until, being no longer able even to stand, we slipped away quietly, and came back to the hotel.

CONTINUED ON PAGE 112

11

ORK STAGED ITS GREATEST PARTY—

TRYING TO REPEAT IT AT HALF-PRICE

ISBET

ONG SHEET COVER OF "THE BOZ WALTZES" PLAYED AT THE BALL

AMERICA: CURATOR OF

BRITISH POLITICAL RELICS

An English observer says our party workings, patronage,

sheriffs, and grand juries are museum pieces from Britain's past

By KEITH KYLE

In exploring the highways and byways of American politics, I have been drawn to the conclusion that there is more real conservation of ancient English institutions in the rich geological strata of American politics—at the state and county level, perhaps, even more than at the federal level—than there is in England itself. Americans come to Britain to see the roots of their political system in the past and find much to inspire them in symbols and relics and ritual and medieval mummery of one sort or another. But to see many historic British institutions working more robustly than they have worked in Britain for years and to rediscover the type of political conflict which characterized so much of British history, Englishmen should go to the New World. Many of the more bewildering and irritating features of American politics—the separation of powers between President and Congress, the odd two-party system which usually fails to polarize opinions—would be far less mysterious to Englishmen if they knew rather more than most of them do about their own political history.

Let me illustrate what I mean by a few concrete examples of institutions of sound English vintage, dead or moribund in England but of great practical importance in the United States. Here are three: the sheriff, the grand jury, the conference committees of Congress.

The sheriff and his posse—the old *posse comitatus* of the statute books—played a central role in Anglo-Saxon, medieval, Tudor, and Stuart local government

and in western cowboy films. Connoisseurs of these will recall the sheriff and his specially sworn-in deputies, who charge frenziedly in the wake of the bad men, until, on the verge of overtaking them, they are obliged to pull up short on the county boundary. Sheriffs—high sheriffs and undersheriffs—do retain some vestigial powers in England; but they have nothing like the important position they used to have and which they still have in American counties. In many of the more decentralized American states "the government" for all practical purposes means the sheriff and the probate judge, both of whom are locally elected politicians. This helps to explain the extreme hostility in heavily Negro-populated counties in the South to letting the Negroes have the vote in any substantial numbers. Every state—even Mississippi—has a white majority over the whole state, but the races are unevenly spread, and in several of the southern states votes for Negroes would probably mean in many counties Negro sheriffs and Negro judges.

In full line with medieval tradition the American sheriff is frequently not only the law enforcement officer, but he is tax assessor and jailer into the bargain. In all these functions he and his deputies must somewhat respect the force of local opinion. When I was last in Wisconsin a deputy sheriff was sacked in the county I was visiting: first, because he had fed margarine to the prisoners—and Wisconsin is a great butter-producing state—and only secondly because state officials wanted to see the prisoners, and the deputy sheriff took two hours to find the key.

A second example, and perhaps a more striking one, of an old English institution thriving in the New World is the grand jury, dead and buried in England by the Administration of Justice (Miscellaneous Provisions) Act, 1933,

and dying on the vine for some time before. This is the old jury of presentment, with origins stretching back to the Henrician reforms of the twelfth century, and even beyond: the group of neighbors specially empaneled to tell of mysterious crimes, hold special inquiries, and indict suspected persons—still the main form of indictment in the United States. The American grand jury meets in private, has powers of subpoena over persons and papers. It has greatly expanded its authority to probe, when so charged by a judge, suspicious patterns of behavior that, when scrutiny is borne down on them, may yield indictments.

My third example is the conference committees of Congress. America is the only democratic country in the world in which the upper house has not lost strength in relation to the lower. Congress has two houses of equal power—if anything the Senate is more powerful than the House of Representatives—in each of which legislation can be initiated. When different measures on the same subject pass the Senate and the House they have to be reconciled; the final wording which goes up for the President's signature is hammered out, often after a great deal of hard bargaining, by managers who are appointed from each of the houses and who meet together in secret session. This is ancient British procedure. The legislation of the House of Lords and the House of Commons used to be reconciled in this way; but this process has died out in England because of the declining power of the House of Lords.

These three instances of English history in American institutions stand out, but there are many other illustrations of my thesis, particularly at the state and local level. There is fee-paying, a central feature of medieval justice. I was fascinated to discover that in Illinois and a few other states the justices of the peace, who are elected politicians, take a commission percentage on the fines they impose; these are the old fruits of justice about

LILI RÉTHI

which early law books waxed witty. And the sheriff's is, in the majority of cases, a fee-paid job. He gets a fee every time he assesses property, conveys a prisoner from jail to the courtroom, and so on. Out of this income he has to meet expenses—maintenance of the jail, hiring of deputy sheriffs and assessors—and he usually ends up with a handsome profit. One rather battered professional politician in a middle western county told me during the 1954 election that his nomination by his party for the office of sheriff was the reward for a lifetime of political drudgery, "shaking hands and ringing doorbells," and that if elected he would clear a profit of $30,000 a year for four years.

All up and down America one comes across local government officials whose titles and duties or absence of them have more meaning to a medievalist than to a student of modern British government; though I do not want to overstate the case and imply that in the preservative American air none of these ancient offices ever expires of inanition. There was an election in April of last year, for example, in a county in Florida in which there were two candidates for the office of constable; one promised that if elected he would find some functions for the office, the other that if elected he would do absolutely nothing at all. The second candidate won—hands down.

The rotten borough, a far-off historical joke in England, does not seem so distant when one comes across the Atlantic. Perhaps there is no complete American equivalent to Old Sarum whose four voters were the butt of every attack on the franchise system in England before the reforms of 1832. But there is one "inhabited town" of forty people which sends a representative to the legislature of Vermont. And a study of the apportionment of state legislatures in general will make the English political historian feel much more at home than in present-day England, with its constituencies scrupulously bounded by an impartial commission according to the arithmetic of population.

Moreover, the states tend to preserve that old-fashioned preference for country over city opinion for which the Duke of Wellington fought so rugged a rear-guard action in the last years of the unreformed Parliament. Before 1832 the two knights who were returned from each

English county, no matter what its population, had infinitely more prestige in Westminster than the mere burgesses from the boroughs, whose numbers were artificially kept low. Borough members would resign from the House in order to contest a county seat that fell vacant. How very English, of pre-Reform Bill vintage, was the spirit of the recent remark by Senator Raymond Gillespie, of the Iowa state senate, who explained his opposition to reapportionment by saying: "I think the people in the rural areas think straighter. We're more like plain Americans. We're not dominated by labor and radicals."

As for the judicial branch of government it is not merely the grand jury that keeps British tradition alive. Until 1947 there was a perfect specimen on American soil of the old English court system, refined through the Middle Ages, whose dilatory glories were so piously tended by Lord Eldon and whose obfuscations were chronicled in Dickens' *Bleak House*. This was in New Jersey, which had the most backward judicial system of all the states and since the new constitution of 1947 now has the most advanced. A member of the constitutional convention which wrought the changes told me that he and his colleagues had to be briefed by medieval historians about the existing structure because it was too ancient and complicated to be understood by the judges themselves. Although New Jersey's judiciary is now streamlined, as the British courts have been for nearly a century, parts of the old English system can still be found in many other states. One can find, as one cannot now in England, separate chancery courts for handling cases in equity. And the use of feudal law in land cases is much more likely to be encountered in an American state than in "the old country." In England practically all remaining feudal law was abolished in 1925 at the instance of a famous lord chancellor who, while at Oxford, had sworn to do away with "the rule in Shelley's case" when his inability to remember it had cost him a coveted academic distinction.

The Supreme Court itself, in some ways the most un-English of American institutions, is yet in a sense a lineal descendant of the *Curia Regis*. It continues the medieval conception of legislation, that of interpreting an existing canon of laws and procedures in the light of a changing society. There was no inevitability about England's choice of the route of the absolute sovereignty of Parliament. Even though the Tudors had developed the principle rather far—with statutes for everything from the establishment of the king at the head of the Church to the boiling of the Bishop of Rochester's cook—it was still possible for Lord Chief Justice Coke, in the reign of James I, to claim that the great principles of common law overrode inconsistent legislation. While England did not take up Coke's cue, America did, and on Coke's interpretation of English constitutional history (which was often faulty as to scholarship) America is in the main line.

The American system of patronage is in the finest and best-pedigreed English tradition, now largely extinct in the land of its origin. The Americans make great use of high-sounding or humble-sounding sinecures as a means of providing public incomes or pensions to dependents for men without whose full-time party activity the political organizations would never keep going. The method will be familiar to students of feudal serjeanties [lands granted under obligations of various personal services to a king or lord] and of eighteenth-century English politics. Readers of Edwin O'Connor's novel, *The Last Hurrah*, about the declining days of a big city boss, will remember that provision is even made for the maintenance in some unexacting office of a court jester—the equivalent, one must suppose, of that twelfth-century Rolland who was given a manor by the king in serjeanty, for which, once a year at the king's feast, "*debuet facere unum saltum, et siffletum et unum bumbulum*" —he must make a jump, a whistle, and a vulgar noise.

Many of the old, picturesque, political sinecures were done away with in England at the very end of the eighteenth century by Edmund Burke and his movement for economical reform. It is a curious thing that, on a visit to Chicago about three years ago, I came across what was termed an economical reform group in the Chicago City Council, one of the most anomaly-ridden bodies in America. Members of this group, headed by Alderman Robert E. Merriam, were challenging items that turned up year after year in the city budget. There was the famous case of the 28 chauffeurs of gas meter readers. The inquisitive reformers asked why gas meter readers could not drive their own cars. They were told that heavy slabs sometimes had to be moved in order to read the meter and a second man was needed. It was pointed out that nearly all the chauffeurs were women. The explanation given was that the chauffeurs were often the wives of the readers and the wives in fact read while the readers moved slabs. It was pointed out that most of the women chauffeurs were widows. It emerged in fact that they were nearly all elderly party officials or widows or dependents of officials; none of them actually drove the cars; they hired drivers at a much smaller fee than they were paid themselves to do the job. This is purest medieval serjeanty. The result of the efforts of the economical reform group was that the council, heavily dominated by party officials, raised the salaries of gas meter readers' chauffeurs.

Political patronage in America and the character of party politics are in fact much what they were in England for by far the greater part of English parliamentary history. It is only in the last hundred years or so that English institutions, unprotected by written constitutions, have changed in revolutionary fashion. Take, for example, the letter from Representative Wright Patman of Texas to one of his constituents, published by the *Reporter* magazine not so long ago: a long recital of all the favors Mr. Patman had done for this man and the jobs he had secured for him and his relatives, ending with a bitter complaint about the political ingratitude with which this assiduity had been rewarded. Change a few names and this could have come straight from the files of that indefatigable eighteenth-century borough-monger, the Duke of Newcastle.

When British students come to study the eighteenth century they have to undergo a prolonged period of intellectual brainwashing—what might be called Namierizing *—which purges their minds of any residual idea that the term "party" as used then had any resemblance to the closely knit, coherent, and disciplined structures of England today. Americans hardly require such a preliminary process. For party politics in America greatly resembles the eighteenth-century variety. There is a passage in John Brooke's new book on the Chatham administration, in which he sets out to invest the eighteenth-century term "party" with some kind of meaning. For the most part he falls back on rivalry over local issues within a county as the reason for sharp elections; the sum total of these results, each in itself having relatively little to do with national affairs, being reflected in the composition of Parliament. The same could be said of Congress. Just as there was no "government party" with a firm majority in the eighteenth-century Parliament—and neither is there in Congress—so there was no precisely definable opposition. There was a prejudice in eighteenth-century Westminster against a "formed opposition" against the Crown, although opposition on particular issues was normal and regular: so in Congress there is no leader of the opposition. The Democratic National Committee, the merest shadow of a national party leadership, attempted, first in 1955, and again during this year, to present a formal front, an alternative leadership to the President. But the Democratic leaders in Congress brushed off the idea as undesirable; they would deal with the President's proposals on their merits, one by one, as they came up.

Although in some ways America is becoming more of a unitary state, it is still, where party organization

* After Sir Lewis Namier, eminent modern historian of the eighteenth century.

is concerned, a loose confederation of states. The really important political leadership is located not in Washington but in the parties of each state; the national parties have to be born anew once every four years, when they meet for a week in national convention to select presidential candidates. It is no accident that it was an American scholar, Professor Wallace Notestein, who made the seminal discovery about the nature of the relationship between the Crown and Parliament under James I which has revolutionized the study of sixteenth- and seventeeth-century political conflicts. Americans are familiar, as Englishmen now are not, with an executive having to deal at arm's length with a legislature, having to get its majorities by manipulating numerous overlapping factions, with the aid of spokesmen who have not themselves drawn up official policy and who may or may not be particularly able or willing to present the Crown's case (or, in America, the President's case) in the most attractive possible light.

In my opinion, after covering Congress for three years, the only really adequate way to report it is in the fashion in which Sir Lewis Namier and his colleagues have been reconstructing eighteenth-century parliaments—to discuss the moves not in terms of parties and fixed groups but in terms of personal and factional shifts and connections, with constant reference to the individual member's state and local political base. This, alas, cannot be done thoroughly by a single correspondent; but it is curious that even in American newspapers the treatment of politics is insufficiently Namierized, moves being treated as if in Congress there were firm parties or groups in the modern European fashion, with use of such phrases as "with a vote cutting right across normal party lines," as if it were usual to have a vote on party lines, whereas in fact it is the rarest of exceptions.

When the Americans formed their Constitution they tried to capture in a written document the essence of the British way of doing things, modified by safeguards and reforms advocated by British radicals since the days of the civil war [between Crown and Parliament]. The Americans did not make a bad job of it, but they locked into the system age-old conflicts which Britons have since resolved by a combination of cabinet government, party discipline, and parliamentary sovereignty. King against Barons, King against Parliament, and now President against Congress: these are conflicts that are inescapable under a system based on the principle of the separation of powers. There are two special characteristics of such a system: first, that the big conflicts are basically insoluble within the existing framework, since the logi-

CONTINUED ON PAGE 126

15

AN IOWA

CHRISTMAS

PAUL ENGLE

*E*very Christmas should begin with the sound of bells, and when I was a child mine always did. But they were sleigh bells, not church bells, for we lived in a part of Cedar Rapids, Iowa, where there were no churches. My bells were on my father's team of horses as he drove up to our horse-headed hitching post with the bobsled that would take us to celebrate Christmas on the family farm ten miles out in the country. My father would bring the team down Fifth Avenue at a smart trot, flicking his whip over the horses' rumps and making the bells double their light, thin jangling over the snow, whose radiance threw back a brilliance like the sound of bells.

There are no such departures any more: the whole family piling into the bobsled with a foot of golden oat straw to lie in and heavy buffalo robes to lie under, the horses stamping the soft snow, and at every motion of their hoofs the bells jingling, jingling. My father sat there with the reins firmly held, wearing a long coat made from the hide of a favorite family horse, the deep chestnut color still glowing, his mittens also from the same hide. It always troubled me as a boy of eight that the horses had so indifferent a view of their late friend appearing as a warm overcoat on the back of the man who put the iron bit in their mouths.

There are no streets like those any more: the snow sensibly left on the road for the sake of sleighs and easy travel. We could hop off and ride the heavy runners as they made their hissing, tearing sound over the packed snow. And along the streets we met other horses, so that we moved from one set of bells to another, from the tiny tinkle of the individual bells on the shafts to the silvery, leaping sound of the long strands hung over the harness. There would be an occasional brass-mounted automobile laboring on its narrow tires and as often as not pulled up the slippery hills by a horse, and we would pass it with a triumphant shout for an awkward nuisance which was obviously not here to stay.

The country road ran through a landscape of little hills and shallow valleys and heavy groves of timber, including one of great towering black walnut trees which were all cut down a year later to be made into gunstocks for the First World War. The great moment was when we left the road and turned up the long lane on the farm. It ran through fields where watermelons were always planted in the summer because of the fine sandy soil, and I could go out and

ILLUSTRATED FOR AMERICAN HERITAGE BY DOUGLAS GORSLINE

break one open to see its Christmas colors of green skin and red inside. My grandfather had been given some of that farm as bounty land for service as a cavalryman in the Civil War.

Near the low house on the hill, with oaks on one side and apple trees on the other, my father would stand up, flourish his whip, and bring the bobsled right up to the door of the house with a burst of speed.

There are no such arrivals any more: the harness bells ringing and clashing like faraway steeples, the horses whinnying at the horses in the barn and receiving a great, trumpeting whinny in reply, the dogs leaping into the bobsled and burrowing under the buffalo robes, a squawking from the hen house, a yelling of "Whoa, whoa," at the excited horses, boy and girl cousins howling around the bobsled, and the descent into the snow with the Christmas basket carried by my mother.

Garsline

While my mother and sisters went into the house, the team was unhitched and taken to the barn, to be covered with blankets and given a little grain. That winter odor of a barn is a wonderfully complex one, rich and warm and utterly unlike the smell of the same barn in summer: the body heat of many animals weighing a thousand pounds and more; pigs in one corner making their dark, brown-sounding grunts; milk cattle still nuzzling the manger for wisps of hay; horses eyeing the newcomers and rolling their deep, oval eyes white; oats, hay, and straw tangy still with the live August sunlight; the manure steaming; the sharp odor of leather harness rubbed with neat's-foot oil to keep it supple; the molasses-sweet odor of ensilage in the silo where the fodder was almost fermenting. It is a smell from strong and living things, and my father always said it was the secret of health, that it scoured out a man's lungs; and he would stand there, breathing deeply, one hand on a horse's rump, watching the steam come out from under the blankets as the team

cooled down from their rapid trot up the lane. It gave him a better appetite, he argued, than plain fresh air, which was thin and had no body to it.

A barn with cattle and horses is the place to begin Christmas; after all, that's where the original event happened, and that same smell was the first air that the Christ Child breathed.

By the time we reached the house, my mother and sisters were wearing aprons and busying in the kitchen, as red-faced as the women who had been there all morning. The kitchen was the biggest room in the house and all family life save sleeping went on there. My uncle even had a couch along one wall where he napped and where the children lay when they were ill. The kitchen range was a tremendous black and gleaming one called a Smoke Eater, with pans bubbling over the holes above the fire box and a reservoir of hot water at the side, lined with dull copper, from which my uncle would dip a basin of water and shave above the sink, turning his lathered face now and then to drop a remark into the women's talk, waving his straight-edged razor as if it were a threat to make them believe him. My job was to go to the woodpile out back and keep the fire burning, splitting the chunks of oak and hickory, watching how cleanly the ax went through the tough wood.

It was a handmade Christmas. The tree came from down in the grove, and on it were many paper ornaments made by my cousins, as well as beautiful ones brought from the Black Forest, where the family had originally lived. There were popcorn balls, from corn planted on the sunny slope by the watermelons, paper horns with homemade candy, and apples from the orchard. The gifts tended to be hand-knit socks, or wool ties, or fancy crocheted "yokes" for nightgowns, tatted collars for blouses, doilies with fancy flower patterns for tables, tidies for chairs, and once I received a brilliantly polished cow horn with a cavalryman crudely but bravely carved on it. And there would usually be a cornhusk doll, perhaps with a prune or walnut for a face, and a gay dress of an old corset-cover scrap with its ribbons still bright. And there were real candles burning with real flames, every guest sniffing the air for the smell of scorching pine needles. No electrically lit tree has the warm and primitive presence of a tree with a crown of living fires over it, suggesting whatever true flame Joseph may have kindled on that original cold night.

There are no dinners like that any more: every item from the farm itself, with no deep freezer, no car for driving into town for packaged food. The pies had been baked the day before, pumpkin, apple, and mince; as we ate them, we could look out the window and see the cornfield where the pumpkins grew, the trees from which the apples were picked. There was cottage cheese, with the dripping bags of curds still hanging from the cold cellar ceiling. The bread had been baked that morning, heating up the oven for the meat, and as my aunt hurried by I could smell in her apron that freshest of all odors with which the human nose is honored—bread straight from the oven. There would be a huge brown crock of beans with smoked pork from the hog butchered every November. We could see, beyond the crock, the broad black iron kettle in a corner of the barnyard, turned upside down, the innocent hogs stopping to scratch on it.

There would be every form of preserve: wild grape from the vines in the grove, crab apple jelly, wild blackberry and tame raspberry, strawberry from the bed in the garden, sweet and sour pickles with dill from the edge of the lane where it grew wild, pickles from the rind of the same watermelon we had cooled in the tank at the milk house and eaten on a hot September afternoon.

Cut into the slope of the hill behind the house, with a little door of its own, was the vegetable cellar, from which came carrots, turnips, cabbages, potatoes, squash. Sometimes my scared cousins were sent there for punishment, to sit in darkness and meditate on their sins; but never on Christmas Day. For days after such an ordeal they could not endure biting into a carrot.

And of course there was the traditional sauerkraut, with flecks of caraway seed. I remember one Christmas Day, when a ten-gallon crock of it in the basement, with a stone weighting down the lid, had blown up, driving the stone against the floor of the parlor, and my uncle had exclaimed, "Good God, the piano's fallen through the floor."

All the meat was from the home place too. Most useful of all, the goose—the very one which had chased me the summer before, hissing and darting out its bill at the end of its curving neck like a feathered snake. Here was the universal bird of an older Christmas: its down was plucked, washed, and hung in bags in the barn to be put into pillows; its awkward body was roasted until the skin was crisp as a fine paper; and the grease from its carcass was melted down, a little camphor added, and rubbed on the chests of coughing children. We ate, slept on, and wore that goose.

I was blessed as a child with a remote uncle from the nearest railroad town, Uncle Ben, who was admiringly referred to as a "railroad man," working the run into Omaha. Ben had been to Chicago; just often enough, as his wife Minnie said with a sniff in her voice, "to ruin the fool, not often enough to teach him anything useful." Ben refused to eat fowl in any form, and as a Christmas token a little pork roast would be put in the oven just for him, always referred to by the hurrying ladies in the kitchen as "Ben's chunk." Ben would make frequent trips to the milk house, returning each time a little redder in the face, usually with one of the men toward whom he had jerked his head. It was not many years before I came to associate Ben's remarkably fruity breath not only with the mince pie, but with the jug I found sunk in the bottom of the cooling tank with a stone tied to its neck. He was a romantic person in my life for his constant travels and for that dignifying term "railroad man," so much more impressive than farmer or lawyer. Yet now I see that he was a short man with a fine natural shyness, giving us knives and guns because he had no children of his own.

And of course the trimmings were from the farm too: the hickory nut cake made with nuts gathered in the grove after the first frost and hulled out by my cousins with yellowed hands; the black walnut cookies, sweeter than any taste; the fudge with butternuts crowding it. In the mornings we would be given a hammer, a flat iron, and a bowl of nuts to crack and pick out for the homemade ice cream.

And there was the orchard beyond the kitchen window, the Wealthy, the Russet, the Wolf with its giant-sized fruit, and an apple romantically called the Northern Spy as if it were a suspicious character out of the Civil War.

All families had their special Christmas food. Ours was called Dutch Bread, made from a dough halfway between bread and cake, stuffed with citron and every sort of nut from the farm—hazel, black walnut, hickory, butternut. A little round one was always baked for me in a Clabber Girl baking soda can, and my last act on Christmas Eve was to put it by the tree so that Santa Claus would find it and have a snack— after all, he'd come a long, cold way to our house. And every Christmas morning, he would have eaten it. My aunt made the same Dutch Bread and we smeared over it the same butter she had been churning from their own Jersey (highest butterfat content) milk that same morning.

To eat in the same room where food is cooked—that is the way to thank the Lord for His abundance. The long table, with its different levels where additions had

Gorsline

been made for the small fry, ran the length of the kitchen. The air was heavy with odors not only of food on plates but of the act of cooking itself, along with the metallic smell of heated iron from the hard-working Smoke Eater, and the whole stove offered us its yet uneaten prospects of more goose and untouched pies. To see the giblet gravy made and poured into a gravy boat, which had painted on its sides winter scenes of boys sliding and deer bounding over snow, is the surest way to overeat its swimming richness.

The warning for Christmas dinner was always an order to go to the milk house for cream, where we skimmed from the cooling pans of fresh milk the cream which had the same golden color as the flanks of the Jersey cows which had given it. The last deed before eating was grinding the coffee beans in the little mill, adding that exotic odor to the more native ones of goose and spiced pumpkin pie. Then all would sit at the table and my uncle would ask the grace, sometimes in German, but later, for the benefit of us ignorant children, in English:

Come, Lord Jesus, be our guest,
Share this food that you have blessed.

There are no blessings like that any more: every scrap of food for which my uncle had asked the blessing was the result of his own hard work. What he took to the Lord for Him to make holy was the plain substance that an Iowa farm could produce in an average year with decent rainfall and proper plowing and manure.

The first act of dedication on such a Christmas was to the occasion which had begun it, thanks to the Child of a pastoral couple who no doubt knew a good deal about rainfall and grass and the fattening of animals. The second act of dedication was to the ceremony of eating. My aunt kept a turmoil of food circulating, and to refuse any of it was somehow to violate the elevated nature of the day. We were there not only to celebrate a fortunate event for mankind, but also to recognize that suffering is the natural lot of men—and to consume the length and breadth of that meal was to suffer! But we all faced the ordeal with courage. Uncle Ben would let out his belt—a fancy Western belt with steer heads and silver buckle—with a snap and a sigh. The women managed better by always getting up from the table and trotting to the kitchen sink or the Smoke Eater or outdoors for some item left in the cold. The men sat there grimly enduring the glory of their appetites.

After dinner, late in the afternoon, the women would make despairing gestures toward the dirty dishes and scoop up hot water from the reservoir at the side of the range. The men would go to the barn and look after the livestock. My older cousin would take his new .22 rifle and stalk out across the pasture with the remark, "I saw that fox just now looking for his Christmas goose." Or sleds would be dragged out and we would slide in a long snake, feet hooked into the sled behind, down the hill and across the westward sloping fields into the sunset. Bones would be thrown to dogs, suet tied in the oak trees for the juncos and winter-defying chickadees, a saucer of skimmed milk set out for the cats, daintily and disgustedly picking their padded feet through the snow, and crumbs scattered on a bird feeder where already the crimson cardinals would be dropping out of the sky like blood. Then back to the house for a final warming-up before leaving.

Gorsline

There was usually a song around the tree before we were all bundled up, many thanks all around for gifts, the basket as loaded as when it came, more so, for leftover food had been piled in it. My father and uncle would have brought up the team from the barn and hooked them into the double shafts of the bobsled, and we would all go out into the freezing air of early evening.

On the way to the door I would walk under a photograph of my grandfather, his cavalry saber hung over it (I had once sneaked it down from the wall and in a burst of gallantry had killed a mouse with it behind the corncrib). With his long white beard he looked like one of the prophets in Hurlbut's illustrated *Story of the Bible,* and it was years before I discovered that he had not been off, as a young man, fighting the Philistines, but the painted Sioux. It was hard to think of that gentle man, whose family had left Germany in protest over military service, swinging that deadly blade and yelling in a cavalry charge. But he had done just that, in some hard realization that sometimes the way to have peace and a quiet life on a modest farm was to go off and fight for them.

And now those bells again as the horses, impatient from their long standing in the barn, stamped and shook their harness, my father holding them back with a soft clucking in his throat and a hard pull on the reins. The smell of wood smoke flavoring the air in our noses, the cousins shivering with cold, "Goodbye, good-bye," called out from everyone, and the bobsled would move off, creaking over the frost-brittle snow. All of us, my mother included, would dig down in the straw and pull the buffalo robes up to our chins. As the horses settled into a steady trot, the bells gently chiming in their rhythmical beat, we would fall half asleep, the hiss of the runners comforting. As we looked up at the night sky through half-closed eyelids, the constant bounce and swerve of the runners would seem to shake the little stars as if they would fall into our laps. But that one great star in the East never wavered. Nothing could shake it from the sky as we drifted home on Christmas.

Paul Engle was born in Iowa in 1908, grew up in Cedar Rapids, and was educated in Iowa schools. Soon after receiving his master's degree from the State University of Iowa he began teaching there. He is now professor of English and conductor of the university's nationally famous poetry workshop.

Fire-eating

At Sumter

Edmund Ruffin

unwittingly pushed

toward ruin the region

whose agricultural

economy he had revived

Ruffin, in his homespun suit adorned with the insignia of the Palmetto Guards, sat for his portrait the day after the surrender of Fort Sumter. The sketches of the fort, drawn by Ruffin in his diary, show the effects of Union guns on this symbol of rebellion.

By ALFRED STEINBERG

In October, 1818, a pale, spindle-legged young Virginia planter stood before the Prince George Agricultural Society and nervously read an essay he had prepared on calcareous manures. Edmund Ruffin was 24 then, small and sickly, with a preposterously long mane that hung far below his shoulders. His delivery was poor, but his eyes burned with zeal and impatience as he told new truths about the use of lime. When he finished speaking, he thanked his listeners and went home. It had been, he disappointedly believed, an academic exercise.

But Ruffin was wrong. Reprinted in a magazine in 1821, this obscure young man's essay in time swept the South and made his name a household word. Expanded into a book, it ran to five editions in the next three decades. Farmers who scoffed at "book agriculture" clamored for it. They began beseeching him for answers to all their farming ills. Former President John Tyler, nearing the sunset of a long career, acclaimed emotionally: "You have done more good to the country than all our political great men put together."

Why all this fuss about Ruffin? At its root lay the agricultural condition of the South. By the end of the

Farmer of the Confederacy

eighteenth century, the soil of the Tidewater district of Virginia had been exhausted, and up and down the Atlantic regions of the South there were similar signs of disaster.

Soil given over for more than a century to intensive single-crop cultivation was no longer productive. In the years following the War of 1812, some of the oldest families began to desert ancestral plantations in a headlong search for rich river bottom land on the frontier. Wagons filled with slaves and piled high with household possessions rutted the narrow roads leading westward. Surveying the situation, John Randolph of Roanoke forecast with his usual sarcasm that the day was not far distant when masters would run away from slaves and be advertised for in the newspapers.

Upon this desperate scene came the wispy figure of Ruffin with a plan for stemming the tide. The scheme was to revive agriculture by scientific farming and thus keep the southern elite from diffusing itself on the wide frontier. Pouring his mind and body into the task, he worked feverishly creating model farms, teaching, coaxing, and threatening southern farmers through an enormous output of speeches and writing until his methods were accepted. Through almost half a century of activity, he was to emerge as the antebellum South's greatest agricultural scientist and as the father of soil chemistry in America. His pioneering theories on bacteriological activities in soil were several decades ahead of his time. So were his proposals for agricultural colleges and a system of county agents for advising farmers.

But there was a tail as well as a head to Ruffin's coin. Slowly his grand purpose began to crystallize. He would prevent the death knell of slavery and make the South strong enough to repel any attacks on its way of life. Whether by manure or guns, it mattered not, so long as the South was saved. Where the scientist left off, the wildest of fire-eaters and secessionists took over. Yankees were as poisonous to Ruffin as sterile soil. He would wipe them off the face of the earth; and he did what he could at the John Brown affair, Fort Sumter, and Manassas. He was the little man who was there, pushing and clawing his beloved South to disaster. He claimed to have fired the first shot of the War Between the States as well as the shot that brought on the Yankee stampede from the First Ma-

nassas. No other doughty warrior could claim as much.

There was nothing in Ruffin's youth to indicate the role he would play in later years. In fact, all indications were that he would never attain the life for which he was being reared—that of a pleasure-loving planter along the James River. Ruffin was the feeblest of infants when he was born in 1794 to a gentleman Virginia landowner named George Ruffin. Although he managed to survive infancy, he was such a puny child that he was pampered and petted as if his days were numbered. He showed no sign of a venturesome spirit, no bent for science, although at ten he proudly announced that he had waded through all of Shakespeare's plays.

Not until he was sixteen was he permitted to leave home. Frail or not, upon the insistence of his parents that he get an education, he enrolled at the College of William and Mary at Williamsburg. Here he revealed such an enormous knack for neglecting his studies that the college authorities ousted him during his first year. Back home once more, he developed a voracious appetite for novels and won a minor reputation for intemperate drinking. At eighteen, to prove he was not a weakling despite his 100 pounds, he enlisted as a private in the first muster of the War of 1812. He managed to survive six months of drill and camp duty, but he grew tired of the boring regimentation and resigned.

It took his father's death and his own marriage to shake Ruffin loose. When he inherited an estate at Coggin's Point on the James River and brought to it his new bride, Susan Travis of Williamsburg, young Ruffin felt obliged for the first time to look beyond his nose. The normal routine of the neighboring planter aristocracy was to ignore farm operations entirely. White supervisors were hired to run the farms and rule the slaves, while the planter-aristocrats engaged freely in politics or in gentlemanly law practice amid a fairly constant round of fox hunts, lavish dinners, and dances.

With a poor formal education and a sudden distaste for the social graces, Ruffin foresaw an idle life ahead unless he found some way to occupy his time. But what was there to do?

To while away his time, he took to walking about his estate. He discussed crops with his supervisor, watched the slaves in the fields, examined the half-stunted grain and the patches of barren ground. And what he observed appalled him.

His soil, like that of his neighbors, was played out. All these planters were leading a life based entirely on economic unreality; all were faced with a proposition that, in time, would impoverish them. Yet, whether from ignorance or despair, they maintained a curtain of silence. Watching his neighbors pursue their spendthrift activities, Ruffin raged: "Like the inhabitants of a city ravaged by the plague, they thought more of present enjoyment than of providing for future wants; and there prevailed generally habits of idleness and improvidence, of pleasure seeking and of neglect of business." He found them a sorry lot; they provided him with a mirror of his own earlier life. When he looked into the possibility of selling his estate, he was astounded to learn that "there was scarcely a proprietor in my neighborhood . . . who did not desire to sell his land, and who was prevented only by the impossibility of finding a purchaser. . . . All wished to sell, none to buy."

Lacking a visible alternative, Ruffin decided to save his inheritance, although he had not the vaguest notion of how to do it. The first glimmering of what he might do came in 1813 when *The Arator*, the agricultural essays of John Taylor of Caroline, appeared in book form.

Hungrily, he plowed through *The Arator* to learn Taylor's secrets. The ideas, he found, were not too difficult to understand. Taylor proclaimed that plowing under vegetable matter before it began to rot would yield an excellent manure for revitalizing soil. He urged raising clover for this purpose, a deep plowing system for all crops, and a bar against permitting cattle to graze in the fields. If this were all there were to successful farming, Ruffin reasoned, his plantation would soon be profitable.

However, following Taylor's precepts, he found that after the first season his land was still unproductive. Nor was the second or the third season any better. "No part of my poor land was more productive than when my labors commenced," he admitted ruefully. As for Taylor's methods, he concluded that they had "proved either profitless, entirely useless, or absolutely and in some cases greatly injurious."

Nevertheless, he felt that he could not give up. There were other agriculturalists who might be of aid. In his search he picked up a copy of Sir Humphrey Davy's *Elements of Agricultural Chemistry*. Although Ruffin knew no chemistry, he was taken with one line in the book: "If on washing a sterile soil it is found to contain the salt of iron, or any other acid matter, it may be ameliorated by the application of quick-lime."

Davy emphasized that lime would convert poisonous sulphates into good manure.

There was first the basic problem of how to go about testing soil for chemicals. In spite of his ignorance of even the rudiments of chemistry, Ruffin plunged into the task of educating himself. He devoured book after book in order to build up understanding.

Unfortunately, when Ruffin finally tested his soil for salts of iron, he found none. If none were present, he brooded, then Davy's theory was down the drain. Perhaps there was something else in the soil that made his land sterile. If it were not mineral, could it be vegetable?

And from this he finally deduced his own theory. There had to be vegetable acids in the soil that made his land sterile. Neutralizing such acidity, lime would convert these poisons into manure and thus build up

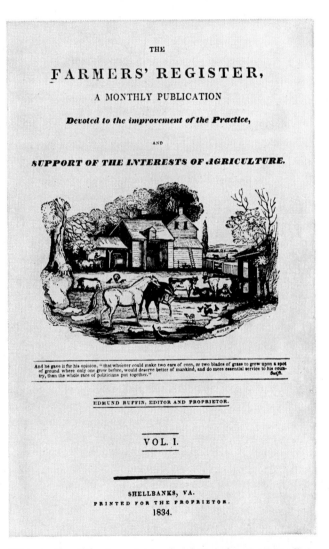

This is the title page from the first volume of Ruffin's Farmers' Register, *hailed as the "best publication on agriculture which this country or Europe has ever produced."*

the soil's fertility. After this was accomplished, John Taylor's idea of using vegetable manures would bring even greater fertility.

Ruffin set about to make careful scientific experiments to prove his theory. When he found large deposits of fossil-shell marl on his land, his plan crystallized. Marl, abundant in Tidewater Virginia, was chemically a mixture of clay and carbonate of lime.

On a strip of land of two and a half acres, he applied about 400 bushels of marl. For purposes of comparison, he planted this section and an adjoining unmarled section with corn. He repeated this process on similar fields planted with wheat. The marl's success was quickly demonstrated. The marl-treated cornfield produced a 45 per cent higher yield than its neighbor. The luxuriant growth of wheat on the marled field showed an even more striking difference.

A gigantic undertaking now began to form in Ruffin's mind. He would broaden his experiment the next year, and if his efforts again proved successful the entire South must be informed of his discovery. There would no longer be any reason for the forced migration of the planter class.

Despite a variety of ailments, he stepped up his pace. He kept detailed records of soil analysis, the use of marl, vegetable manuring, crop developments, and farming costs. At the end of the season, when his expectations were more than fulfilled, he rushed to tell the Prince George Agricultural Society about his work. And when there was no immediate rejoicing he returned to Coggin's Point to broaden his experiments further.

As his profits increased, Ruffin turned his plantation into a show place. He wisely believed that others would be more receptive to theories seen in successful application. Despite a poor speaking voice and a painful shyness, he took every opportunity to explain his work at meetings of farmers. He talked about soil bacteria, a subject that seemed wholly implausible in his day. He began writing articles for newspapers and magazines and chided readers for not using marl. He admitted that lime had been used in Europe for centuries, but there had been no tangible theory behind its use. No one before him had mentioned the harmful vegetable acids that had to be neutralized.

It would be a gross error to say that Ruffin's propagandizing met with early success and that he was catapulted to fame. Some old planter families considered him a meddlesome crackpot. "Ruffin's folly," they labeled his marl. Neighboring planters held their sides from laughter as the young upstart tried to explain his theory. When he talked about his own

Marlbourne, from an old photograph, was a "prospect of rare beauty." Ruffin bought it because it was also "highly susceptible of improvement and greatly in want of it."

original method for determining how much carbonate of lime lay in any given soil, they sneered to his face. And when they watched the heavy loads of books from abroad being delivered to Beechwood Mansion, they winked to each other. Ruffin never forgave them for their derision: "Most farmers are determined *not* to understand anything, however simple it may be, which relates to chemistry," he charged.

But the indifference and scorn he met only fired his determination. The days and the years passed. In 1821 the *American Farmer* reprinted his essay on marl. The editors called it the "first systematic attempt . . . to examine into the real composition of the soils." Here was his first step forward. Farmers from far off read it. Out of curiosity many wrote him for further information. Others found reason to travel past Coggin's Point to see for themselves.

Politics seemed a good way to push himself faster. In 1823 he won election to the Virginia Senate, and he served three years at Williamsburg with the hope of spreading his farming doctrines. But he found politics a poor springboard for what he had in mind. The frenzied national election of 1824 obliterated all local issues, and for some time to come its repercussions reaped the major share of newspaper interest. When he left politics Ruffin vowed never to have anything further to do with public office.

In 1833 he started his own monthly publication, the *Farmers' Register*. As his guide he took the saying from Swift, ". . . that whoever could make two ears of corn, or two blades of grass, to grow upon a spot of ground where only one grew before, would deserve better of mankind, and do more essential service to his country than the whole race of politicians put together."

His magazine proved a whopping success. Within a year it became the farming bible from Georgia to

CONTINUED ON PAGE 114

"THE GRAY-EYED MAN OF DESTINY"

By EDWARD S. WALLACE

William Walker, shown above at the start of his filibustering career, is savagely immortalized in the unique monument at right, which stands in San José, the capital of Costa Rica. It shows the beaten Walker being driven off by the five angry, righteous republics of Central America.

26

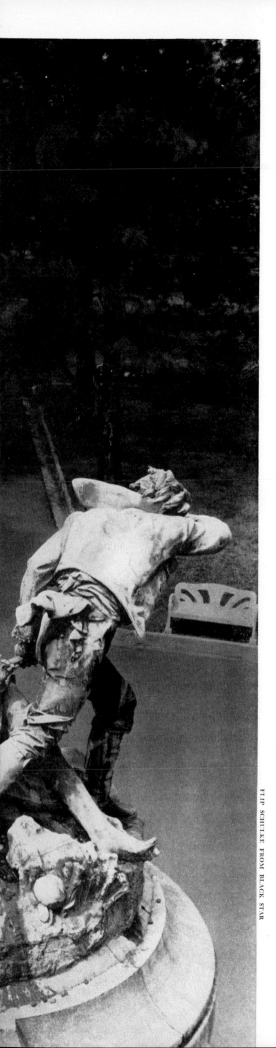

The daring epic of the filibusters reached

a lurid climax when little William Walker

captured the sovereign state of Nicaragua

For a young American who wanted excitement and adventure along with a chance to get rich quick, the United States of a hundred years ago offered plentiful opportunity. The adjustment of the Oregon boundary with Great Britain in 1846, the decisive victory over Mexico and the acquisition of about half the territory of that unfortunate republic in 1848, and then, almost immediately afterward, the discovery of gold in California—all these opened avenues of adventure for men of mettle and daring.

There was, as well, for the truly reckless or the desperate, an even more alluring outlet than settling new lands or prospecting for gold, and this had the promise that the gold they were after had already been mined. The men who followed this highly dangerous way were called filibusters—a term used then in its most masculine sense, meaning freebooters, and not, as now, windy and obstructive politicians. These exuberant daredevils tried to seize by force of arms various Latin American countries, usually with the sincere belief that they were the instruments of the "Manifest Destiny" of the United States to acquire and civilize the chaotic and wartorn republics to the south.

The extremists of this imperialistic faith fervently believed that the United States, following its destiny, would eventually annex the entire Western Hemisphere from the Arctic snows to Cape Horn. And in 1856 they came very close indeed to success in Nicaragua, when William Walker made himself president of that harassed republic, the only time in history a native-born American has become the head of another sovereign nation. If Walker had then acted with discretion the whole history of the Americas might have been changed, for he and most of the other rampaging filibusters were proslavery southerners whose enthusiasm for American expansion was linked with the desire to gain new lands for that "peculiar institution."

The times favored a spirit of enthusiastic nationalism and an unshakable conviction of the superiority of the United States over all other nations. Few Americans then cared what the rest of the world thought of them—what they thought of the rest of the world was all that mattered. Even the federal government caught the fever of expansion; the Administration of President Franklin Pierce (1853-57) approached Russia about the purchase of Alaska, broached the matter of annexation with the king of the Hawaiian Islands, attempted to buy Cuba from Spain, and made overtures toward

27

the purchase of a large naval base in the Dominican Republic. None of these efforts succeeded at the time, however, and the only tangible gain of territory was the land acquired along the Mexican border by the Gadsden Purchase of 1853.

Most of the filibusters, who sought to gain by force what their government could not acquire by diplomacy, were men of the frontier with a good leavening of Mississippi River men of the "half-horse-half-alligator" type. There was a certain proportion of barflies and drifters from the slums of the big cities, but the officers and hard core of these adventurers must have been a magnificent lot of men, the pick of the frontiersmen of the time. An English explorer wrote of some of William Walker's followers in Nicaragua: "Tall, upright, broad-shouldered men they were nearly all. Their heads were well set on, hands and feet small, muscles like iron . . . the very pick of the Western States—men highly thought of even there for reckless daring. . . . They were simply the most good-natured, good-tempered fellows I ever met with."

The filibusters used two general methods of operation. The first was a slam-bang landing on the coast of one of the southern republics and the proclamation of a new government with the invaders holding all the key offices. But this forthright procedure was so blatantly crude and smacked so of piracy that it outraged public opinion not only in the country attacked but throughout the world; it never gained more than the initial local success of surprise.

The more successful method was for a group of Americans to enlist as a distinct corps in one of the warring factions in the new Spanish-speaking republics. For a while these volunteers were eagerly sought by the revolutionary leaders because of their superb fighting qualities; they were recruited by promises of sizable tracts of land—the idea being that these soldiers of fortune, after victory was attained, would settle down as solid citizens to enjoy the rewards of victory. The danger, however, was that these adventurers, as a compact and disciplined body, would seize the govern-

ment itself. This is exactly what William Walker and his followers accomplished in Nicaragua, in the filibuster which came nearest to permanent success.

Walker's filibustering career had begun two years before—with a fiasco. In the autumn of 1853 he had descended with forty-odd followers on Lower California and proclaimed it an independent republic with himself as president. When reinforcements arrived he extended his sway on paper by a proclamation annexing the neighboring state of Sonora to his newly established nation and the San Francisco newspaper *Alta California* aptly noted, "It would have been just as cheap and easy to have annexed the whole of Mexico at once, and would have saved the trouble of making future proclamations." The whole affair was ridicu-

A filibuster attack on the enemy town of Rivas is shown in this 1856 sketch. Walker's favorite battle tactic was a slam-bang raid, designed to gain the central plaza.

lous on the surface but not so funny to some of the people immediately in Walker's way, for he had a deadly determination and never hesitated to execute anyone who obstructed his purpose. Chased out of Lower California, he managed to lead 33 surviving followers back to safety across the border below San Diego on May 8, 1854, which happened to be his thirtieth birthday.

But from this initial defeat Walker was to go on to become the grand master of the filibusters. One would imagine that the leader of such hard-bitten daredevils must have been a man of splendid physique and overwhelming personality. But Walker was nothing of the sort. He was about as innocuous looking as a man could be. Only about five feet, five inches in height, he weighed just over a hundred pounds. His hair and eyebrows were tow-white and his pale face was covered with the freckles which usually go with such coloring. His expression was heavy and he was taciturn to an extreme, but when he spoke he gained attention with the first word uttered. His eyes were his striking features; all noticed their piercing gray coldness and he became known as "the gray-eyed man of destiny."

Born in Nashville, Tennessee, in 1824 of Scotch-Irish ancestry, Walker had studied medicine in Europe but turned to the law in Nashville and New Orleans upon his return. Then he became a journalist and moved to California, where he edited a newspaper in San Francisco, but later he practiced law again in Marysville until in October, 1853, he sailed with 45

smoking volcanoes had so carried away an early English monk that he had called it "Mahomet's Paradise." The little country had achieved a shaky independence after the downfall of the Mexican emperor in 1823, but ever since had been kept in turmoil by civil warfare. Nicaragua had a special importance for Americans, in these years between the Gold Rush and the Golden Spike, because through it ran the favored route to California—a relatively comfortable passage from one ocean to the other by river and lake boat and a short stretch of road.

Walker's first move was to gain control of this Transit route, which would give him his vital supply line for recruits and equipment from the United States. On a sunny June morning he assembled his little army outside the Legitimist (i.e., Conservative) stronghold of Rivas, which controlled the road section of the Transit route, and about noon he led them on a reckless frontal charge into the town.

FROM *Frank Leslie's Illustrated Newspaper*, 1856

After the attack on Rivas, which ended in retreat, the filibusters take their rest in a battered building. They usually left their enemy too demoralized to pursue them.

At the first shots, his native allies turned tail and left the fifty-odd Americans to fight ten times their numbers. The invaders met a steady and deadly fire as they charged toward the central plaza with wild yells and cheers (the usual head-on tactics of filibusters) and were soon forced to take shelter in several adobe houses where they were surrounded by the enemy. The Legitimists then set fire to the sheltering houses and an immediate retreat became imperative to save the survivors. The Americans sallied forth with cheers and shouts and, before the enemy could meet this unexpected offensive, pushed through the streets to the outskirts of the town. Several of the wounded were too seriously hurt to move, and these were immediately butchered by the Legitimists and their bodies burned. The enemy losses, however, were ten times those of the Americans, and thereafter no sober natives ever wanted to shoot it out at close range with the gringos.

It was a badly beaten group of survivors who reassembled in a cacao plantation outside the town. But Walker got them safely back to their base and in August led them on another foray against the enemy

followers from San Francisco for his invasion of Lower California.

His first humiliating failure in that expedition taught Walker a few lessons but in no way cured him of the filibustering fever. In 1855 he was off again, this time to Nicaragua. There, instead of making a rash and forthright landing, he gained entry as the leader of a band of soldier-colonists who were to serve under the banner of the Outs (who happened to be the Liberals) in the current revolution. His followers became citizens of the country by a simple declaration of intention and were promised grants of land when their newly adopted cause won victory.

In Nicaragua Walker found a green and fertile land whose fragrant orange groves, sparkling lakes, and

CONTINUED ON PAGE 123

29

"We were there, waiting–"

The repulse of Pickett's charge, described in a little-known

account written shortly after the battle by a Union officer

Frank Aretas Haskell

An introduction by BRUCE CATTON

One of the genuine but little-known classics of Civil War literature is a book called *The Battle of Gettysburg*, written by a Northern soldier named Frank Aretas Haskell. Haskell fought in the battle, and less than two weeks after the fighting ceased he wrote a detailed account of what he had seen and experienced and sent the manuscript to his brother, back in Wisconsin.

Haskell had seen and experienced a good deal, for he was an aide on the staff of Brigadier General John Gibbon, commander of the 2nd Division of the Army of the Potomac's Second Army Corps; and it was this division which held the ground against which the most famous assault in American military history was directed—the charge of 15,000 Confederates led by Major General George Pickett, on the afternoon of the third day of the fight. Haskell was at storm center throughout the action, and when he wrote his manuscript the heat of battle was still on him; the town of Gettysburg was still full of wounded men, and the fearful debris of battle still littered its fields.

The book had a curious history. Haskell's brother offered the manuscript to the editor of a small-town paper, who found it far too long for his pages. Some fifteen years later the brother had it printed in pamphlet form, for private distribution. In 1898 an abbreviated version was published as part of the history of

On the facing page is a depiction of the climactic struggle at "the angle," taken from Paul Philippoteaux's epic painting. Pickett's men have broken through the Union line and overrun Cushing's guns, with Unionists rallying at left.

the class of 1854, Dartmouth College—Haskell's own class. This version was reprinted in 1908 by the Commandery of Massachusetts, Military Order of the Loyal Legion of the United States; and the full, unabridged version was printed shortly thereafter under the auspices of the Wisconsin History Commission, in an edition of 2,500 copies. It quickly became a standard reference work for students of the battle, but the general reader rarely saw it.

Now, 94 years after it was written, *The Battle of Gettysburg* is being made available to everyone, in an unabridged edition which is to be published shortly by the Houghton Mifflin Company of Boston. By special arrangement with this publisher, AMERICAN HERITAGE is presenting herewith an excerpt from that part of the book which deals specifically with the repulse of Pickett's charge. (The book as a whole covers the entire battle, which lasted three days, from July 1 through July 3, 1863.)

Haskell himself never saw his narrative in print, for he did not survive the war. Born in Vermont in 1828, he had gone to Madison, Wisconsin, immediately after his graduation from college and had entered the practice of law. When the Civil War broke out he promptly enlisted, and on June 20, 1861, he was commissioned first lieutenant in Company I of the 6th Wisconsin Infantry. This regiment was sent east that summer, and in the spring of 1862, along with the 2nd and 7th Wisconsin and the 19th Indiana regiments (to which, a bit later, was added the 24th Michigan), it became a unit in what was to be one of the most distinguished combat outfits in the Army of the Potomac, the celebrated "Iron Brigade."

This brigade was commanded by Brigadier General John Gibbon, a tough West Pointer in his mid-thirties, who promptly made Lieutenant Haskell an aide on his staff. The two served with the brigade in the battles of Gainesville, Second Bull Run, South Mountain, and Antietam, and in the fall of 1862, when Gibbon was raised to divisional command, he saw to it that Haskell remained on his staff. Haskell stayed with him through Fredericksburg, Chancellorsville, and Gettysburg and won both Gibbon's professional admiration and personal affection. In his report on Gettysburg, Gibbon wrote that Haskell had distinguished himself in every battle "by his conspicuous coolness and bravery," and added: "It has always been a source of regret to me that our military system offers no plan for rewarding his merit and services as they deserve."

The reward came shortly after this. Gibbon was wounded at Gettysburg, and after serving for some months on the staff of the general who replaced him, Haskell was sent to Wisconsin and made colonel of the newly organized 36th Wisconsin Infantry. In the spring of 1864 this regiment was assigned to the Army of the Potomac—Gibbon, by now restored to duty, arranged to get it in his division—and in the battle of Cold Harbor, on June 3, 1864, Haskell was killed leading his regiment in a hopeless assault on the Confederate entrenchments. Informed of his death, Gibbon remarked that he had lost his best friend and that the Army of the Potomac had lost one of its best soldiers.

The reader of Haskell's narrative needs to remember that it was written without benefit of the backward glance and without those inevitable revisions that grow out of long reflection and fuller knowledge. Haskell expresses all of the prejudices which an ardent officer in a hot combat unit might be expected to have, both toward other units in his own army and toward the enemy against whom he was fighting. He had, for example, nothing but contempt for the luckless Eleventh Army Corps in the Army of the Potomac; it was badly mauled at Gettysburg, just as had been the case at Chancellorsville two months earlier, and Haskell wrote it off as a half-hearted group. He also had scant use for such Union officers as Major General Daniel Sickles and Major General Abner Doubleday, and when he wrote about the battle he saw no reason to disguise his feelings.

In addition, Haskell was (naturally enough) red-hot for the Union, and the Confederates were in his eyes no better than outright traitors. The word "Rebel," as he used it, was meant as a word of bitter criticism, and although he was ready to admit that the Southern-

ers were very valiant soldiers—no veteran in the Army of the Potomac was in any doubt on that point—he was not disposed to give them credit for anything else.

In his book, Haskell covers the entire battle of Gettysburg, even though he himself missed the action of the first day.

The great three-day fight began shortly after dawn on July 1, on the ridges west of the town, when advancing Confederate infantry in Lieutenant General A. P. Hill's Third Corps collided with Union cavalry. Major General George Gordon Meade, who had just taken command of the Army of the Potomac, had his army spread out over a considerable area, trying to find Lee's army and bring it to battle, and his First Corps, led by Major General John F. Reynolds, was nearing Gettysburg when the firing started. Reynolds brought his troops into town fast, got to the western ridges, and the battle began. Reynolds was killed, but his troops held their ground—Gibbon's old Iron Brigade was in the thick of the action and suffered fearful casualties—and toward midday reinforcements arrived in the shape of Major General Oliver Otis Howard and the Eleventh Corps, which promptly took position north of town.

The fortunes of war were with the Confederates that day. Lee's Second Corps, under Lieutenant General Richard Ewell—Stonewall Jackson's old troops, these—came into town from the north and northeast, and since Confederate army corps were a great deal larger than Union corps (although there were fewer of them) Lee had a powerful numerical advantage. The Union First and Eleventh Corps were driven from their positions with heavy losses, and as the day ended they took position on Cemetery and Culp's hills, south of Gettysburg, and awaited developments.

On July 2 Lee had most of his army on hand, while a good part of Meade's was still on the road. Lee attacked Culp's Hill with Ewell's corps, and struck the extreme left of Meade's line, at the Round Top hills, with Lieutenant General James B. Longstreet's corps, winning a good deal of ground and knocking the Federal Third Corps completely out of action, but failing to drive the Unionists from Cemetery Ridge, the rounded stretch of high ground that goes south from dominant Cemetery Hill. Both armies remained in position overnight, and when July 3 came it was clear to everyone that the climactic assault of the battle was in the making. At a conference late on the evening of July 2, Meade had remarked that if Lee attacked on the third he would strike Gibbon's front.

That part of Haskell's story which is printed here picks up the situation at dawn on July 3, with Gibbon's division waiting on the crest of Cemetery Ridge for the action which everybody was sure would come.

THE THIRD DAY

AT GETTYSBURG

By FRANK ARETAS HASKELL

First lieutenant on Brigadier General John Gibbon's staff, at Gettysburg;

later colonel of the 36th Wisconsin; killed at Cold Harbor.

As the sun arose to-day, the clouds became broken, and we had once more glimpses of sky, and fits of sunshine—a rarity, to cheer us. From the crest, save to the right of the Second Corps, no enemy, not even his outposts could be discovered, along all the position where he so thronged upon the Third Corps yesterday. The men were roused early, in order that the morning meal might be out of the way in time for whatever should occur. Then ensued the hum of an army, not in ranks, chatting in low tones, and running about and jostling among each other, rolling and packing their blankets and tents.

They looked like an army of rag-gatherers, while shaking these very useful articles of the soldier's outfit, for you must know that rain and mud in conjunction have not had the effect to make them clean, and the wear and tear of service have not left them entirely whole. But one could not have told by the appearance of the men, that they were in battle yesterday, and were likely to be again to-day. They packed their knapsacks, boiled their coffee and munched their hard bread, just as usual—just like old soldiers who know what campaigning is; and their talk is far more con-

cerning their present employment—some joke or drollery—than concerning what they saw or did yesterday.

The dispositions to-day upon the left are as follows:

The Second and Third Divisions of the Second Corps are in the position of yesterday; then on the left come Doubleday's—the Third Division and Col. Stannard's brigade of the First Corps; then the First Division of the Second Corps; then the Third Corps, temporarily under the command of Hancock, since Sickles' wound. Note well the position of the Second and Third Divisions of the Second Corps—it will become important. There are nearly six thousand men and officers in these two Divisions here upon the field, who occupy a line of about a thousand yards. The most of the way along this line upon the crest was a stone fence, constructed of small, rough stones, a good deal of the way badly pulled down, but the men had improved it and patched it with rails from the neighboring fences, and with earth, so as to render it in many places a very passable breastwork against musketry and flying fragments of shells.

These works are so low as to compel the men to kneel or lie down generally to obtain cover. Near the right of the Second Division, and just by a little group of trees, this stone fence made a right angle, and extended thence to the front, about twenty or thirty yards, where with another less than a right angle it followed along the crest again.

[*The "little group of trees" mentioned by Haskell was, and remains, one of the landmarks of the battlefield. Situated near the center of the Second Corps line, it was the guide for the men in Pickett's charge; they aimed at it, they got to it, and a good many of them died near it. The trees, or their descendants, are still there, enclosed by a little iron fence, and today's visitor can see them; and in front of them there is the old stone wall, making an angle which, to the men who fought at Gettysburg, was "the" angle. A great many young men lost their lives in and about the trees and the angle, and a visitor to the spot somehow can feel their presence there.*]

The lines were conformed to these breastworks and to the nature of the ground upon the crest, so as to occupy the most favorable places, to be covered, and still be able to deliver effective fire upon the enemy should he come there. In some places a second line was so posted as to be able to deliver its fire over the heads of the first line behind the works; but such formation was not practicable all of the way. But all the force of these two divisions was in line, in position, without reserves, and in such a manner that every man of them could have fired his piece at the same instant.

I could not help wishing all the morning that this line of the two divisions of the Second Corps was stronger; it was, so far as numbers constitute strength, the weakest part of our whole line of battle. What if, I thought, the enemy should make an assault here today, with two or three heavy lines—a great overwhelming mass; would he not sweep through that thin six thousand?

But I was not General Meade, who alone had power to send other troops there; and he was satisfied with that part of the line as it was. He was early on horseback this morning, and rode along the whole line, looking to it himself and with glass in hand sweeping the woods and fields in the direction of the enemy, to see if aught of him could be discovered. His manner was calm and serious, but earnest. There was no arrogance of hope, or timidity of fear discernible in his face; but you would have supposed he would do his duty conscientiously and well and would be willing to abide the result. You would have seen this in his face.

The enemy, so far as we could see, was very quiet all the morning. Occasionally the outposts would fire

a little, and then cease. Movements would be discovered which would indicate the attempt on the part of the enemy to post a battery. Our Parrotts would send a few shells to the spot, then silence would follow.

[*The Parrotts mentioned by Haskell were rifled field pieces with heavy iron bands shrunk over the breach. For field artillery they came in 10-pound and 20-pound sizes—meaning that they fired shell of that weight, with a caliber of approximately three inches. The Napoleons mentioned in the following paragraph were brass smooth-bores of about 4.5 inches caliber; their range was much less than that of the Parrotts, but for close action they were extremely effective. Firing canister—which meant that they were loaded with tin cans full of round lead pellets—they were like sawed-off shotguns of stupendous size, and against closely-ranked infantry at ranges of 250 yards or less they were simply murderous.*]

Eleven o'clock came. Not a sound of a gun or musket can be heard on all the field; the sky is bright, with only the white fleecy clouds floating over from the West. The July sun streams down its fire upon the bright iron of the muskets in stacks upon the crest, and the dazzling brass of the Napoleons. The army lolls and longs for the shade, of which some get a hand's breadth, from a shelter tent stuck upon a ramrod. The silence and sultriness of a July noon are supreme.

Now it so happened that just about this time of day a very original and interesting thought occurred to Gen. Gibbon and several of his staff; that it would be a very good thing, and a very good time, to have something to eat. Of the absolute quality of what we had to eat, I could not pretend to judge, but I think an unprejudiced person would have said of the bread that it was good; so of the potatoes before they were boiled. Of the chickens he would have questioned their age, but they were large and in good *running* order. The toast was good, and the butter. General Hancock is of course invited to partake, and without delay we commence operations. We were just well at it when General Meade rode down to us from the line, accompanied by one of his staff, and by General Gibbon's invitation, they dismounted and joined us. Fortunate to relate, there was enough cooked for us all, and from General Meade to the youngest second lieutenant we all had a most hearty and well relished dinner. Of the "past" we were "secure." The Generals ate, and after, lighted cigars, and under the flickering shade of a very small tree, discoursed of the incidents of yesterday's battle and of the probabilities of today.

And so the time passed on, each General now and then dispatching some order or message by an officer or orderly, until about half-past twelve, when all the Generals, one by one, first General Meade, rode off their several ways, and General Gibbon and his staff alone remained.

We dozed in the heat, and lolled upon the ground, with half-open eyes. Time was heavy and for want of something better to do, I yawned, and looked at my watch. It was five minutes before one o'clock. I returned my watch to its pocket, and thought possibly that I might go to sleep, and stretched myself upon the ground accordingly. My attitude and purpose were those of the General and the rest of the staff.

What sound was that? There was no mistaking it. The distinct sharp sound of one of the enemy's guns, square over to the front, caused us to open our eyes and turn them in that direction, when we saw directly above the crest the smoke of the bursting shell, and heard its noise. In an instant, before a word was spoken, as if that was the signal gun for general work, loud, startling, booming, the report of gun after gun in rapid succession smote our ears and their shells plunged down and exploded all around us.

We sprang to our feet. In briefest time the whole Rebel line to the West was pouring out its thunder and its iron upon our devoted crest. The wildest confusion for a few moments obtained sway among us. The shells came bursting all about. The servants ran terror-stricken for dear life and disappeared. The horses, hitched to the trees or held by the slack hands of orderlies, neighed out in fright, and broke away and plunged riderless through the fields.

The General at the first had snatched his sword, and started on foot for the front. I called for my horse; nobody responded. I found him tied to a tree, near by, eating oats, with an air of the greatest composure, which under the circumstances, even then struck me as exceedingly ridiculous. He alone, of all beasts or men near was cool. I am not sure but that I learned a lesson then from a horse. General Gibbon's

groom has just mounted his horse and is starting to take the General's horse to him, when the flying iron meets him and tears open his breast. He drops dead and the horses gallop away. No more than a minute since the first shot was fired, and I am mounted and riding after the General. The mighty din that now rises to heaven and shakes the earth is not all of it the voice of the rebellion; for our guns, the guardian lions of the crest, quick to awake when danger comes, have opened their fiery jaws and begun to roar.

I overtake the General half way up to the line. Before we reach the crest his horse is brought by an orderly. Leaving our horses just behind a sharp declivity of the ridge, on foot we go up among the batteries. How the long streams of fire spout from the guns, how the rifled shells hiss, how the smoke deepens and rolls. The men of the infantry have seized their arms, and behind their works, behind every rock, in every ditch, wherever there is any shelter, they hug the ground, silent, quiet, unterrified, little harmed.

[*General Lee had a long rank of guns in line, and all of these opened fire in an attempt to soften the Union line for Pickett's charge. The Union guns instantly replied, and for an hour or thereabouts the greatest artillery duel yet seen on the American continent was waged. The fire was so intense and the racket was so terrific that Union gunners confessed afterward that they could hardly hear the noise their own guns made. The Union line might have been obliterated by the bombardment except for the fact that the Confederate gunners for some reason were firing just a little too high. Most of their shell exploded on the reverse slope of Cemetery Ridge.*]

The enemy's guns now in action are in position at their front of the woods. A hundred and twenty-five rebel guns, we estimate, are now active, firing twenty-four pound, twenty, twelve and ten-pound projectiles, solid shot and shells, spherical, conical, spiral. The enemy's fire is chiefly concentrated upon the position

Major General George Gordon Meade, U.S.A.

of the Second Corps. From the Cemetery to Round Top, with over a hundred guns, and to all parts of the enemy's line, our batteries reply.

Who can describe such a conflict as is raging around us? To say that it was like a summer storm, with the crash of thunder, the glare of lightning, the shrieking of the wind, and the clatter of hailstones, would be weak. The thunder and lightning of these two hundred and fifty guns and their shells, whose smoke darkens the sky, are incessant, all pervading, in the air above our heads, on the ground at our feet, remote, near, deafening, ear-piercing, astounding; and these hailstones are massy iron, charged with exploding fire. And there is little of human interest in a storm; it is an absorbing element of this. You may see flame and smoke, and hurrying men, and human passion at a great conflagration; but they are all earthly and nothing more. These guns are great infuriate demons, not of the earth, whose mouths blaze with smoky tongues of living fire, and whose murky breath, sulphur-laden, rolls around them and along the ground, the smoke of Hades. These grimy men, rushing, shouting, their souls in frenzy, plying the dusky globes and the igniting spark, are in their league, and but their willing ministers.

We thought that at the second Bull Run, at the Antietam and at Fredericksburg on the 13th of December, we had heard heavy cannonading; they were but holiday salutes compared with this. Besides the great ceaseless roar of the guns, which was but the background of the others, a million various minor sounds engaged the ear. The projectiles shriek long and sharp. They hiss, they scream, they growl, they sputter; all sounds of life and rage; and each has its different note, and all are discordant. We see the solid shot strike axle, or pole, or wheel, and the

Lieutenant General James Longstreet, C.S.A.

tough iron and heart of oak snap and fly like straws. And these shot and shells have no respect for men. We see the poor fellows hobbling back from the crest, or, unable to do so, pale and weak, lying on the ground with the mangled stump of an arm or leg, dripping their lifeblood away; or with a cheek torn open or a shoulder mashed. And many, alas! hear not the roar as they stretch upon the ground with upturned faces and open eyes, though a shell should burst at their very ears. Their ears and their bodies this instant are only mud.

We watched the shells bursting in the air, as they came hissing in all directions. Their flash was a bright gleam of lightning radiating from a point, giving place in the thousandth part of a second to a small, white, puffy cloud, like a fleece of the lightest, whitest wool. These clouds were very numerous. We could not often see the shell before it burst; but sometimes, as we faced towards the enemy, and looked above our heads, the approach would be heralded by a prolonged hiss, which always seemed to me to be a line of something tangible, terminating in a black globe, distinct to the eye, as the sound had been to the ear. The shell would seem to stop, and hang suspended in the air an instant, and then vanish in fire and smoke and noise.

We saw the missiles tear and plow the ground. All in rear of the crest for a thousand yards, as well as among the batteries, was the field of their blind fury. Ambulances, passing down the Taneytown road with wounded men, were struck. The hospitals near this road were riddled. The house which was General Meade's headquarters was shot through several times, and a great many horses of officers and orderlies were lying dead around it. The percussion shells would strike, and thunder, and scatter the earth and their whistling fragments; the Whitworth bolts would pound and ricochet, and bowl far away sputtering, with the sound of a mass of hot iron plunged in water; and the great solid shot would smite the unresisting ground with a sounding "thud," as the strong boxer crashes his iron fist into the jaws of his unguarded adversary.

[*The Whitworth bolts referred to by Haskell came from a few artillery pieces imported from England: Whitworth guns, breech-loaders, with a range of four or five miles, which fired hexagonal shells out of barrels which were hexagonal in cross section, twisted to give the missiles the effect of rifling. The shells made a horrendous noise in flight, and although they were no more effective than those of the other field pieces— Civil War artillerists had not yet learned the trick of indirect fire, and the Whitworths had more range than could profitably be used—troops on the receiving end of such fire had come to detest the weapons, and hugged the ground intently when Whitworth projectiles came over. Technically, a bolt from a field piece was a solid shot, but Whitworth missiles were uniformly given that name even though they usually carried a charge of high explosive.*]

Such were some of the sights and sounds of this great iron battle of missiles. An hour has droned its flight since first the war began. There is no sign of weariness or abatement on either side. So long, it seemed, that the din and crashing around began to appear the normal condition of nature there, and fighting man's element.

The General proposed to go among the men and over to the front of the batteries, so at about two o'clock he and I started. We went down in front of the line some two hundred yards, and as the smoke had a tendency to settle upon a higher plain than where we were, we could see near the ground distinctly all over the fields. No infantry was in sight, save the skirmishers, and they stood silent and motionless— a row of gray posts through the field on one side confronted by another of blue. Under the grateful shade of some elm trees, where we could see much of the field, we made seats of the ground and sat down.

On either crest we could see the great flaky streams of fire, and they seemed numberless, of the opposing guns, and their white banks of swift, convolving smoke; but the sound of the discharges was drowned in the universal ocean of sound. Over all the valley the smoke, a sulphury arch, stretched its lurid span; and through it always, shrieking on their unseen courses, thickly flew a myriad iron death. With our grim horizon on all sides round toothed thick with battery flame, under that dissonant canopy of warring shells, we sat and heard in silence. What other expression had we that was not mean, for such an awful universe of battle?

Half-past two o'clock, an hour and a half since the commencement, and still the cannonade did not in the least abate; but soon thereafter some signs of weariness and a little slacking of fire began to be apparent on both sides. The General and I started to return, passing towards the left of the division, and crossing the ground where the guns had stood. Our infantry was still unshaken, and in all the cannonade suffered very little. The batteries had been handled much more severely. Guns had been dismounted. A great many caissons, limbers and carriages had been destroyed, and usually from ten to twenty-five men to each battery had been struck, at least along our part of the crest. Altogether the fire of the enemy

General Robert Edward Lee, C.S.A.

had injured us much; the scenes that met our eyes on all hands among the batteries were fearful.

All things must end, and the great cannonade was no exception. In the number of guns active at one time, and in the duration and rapidity of their fire, this artillery engagement, up to this time, must stand alone and pre-eminent in this war. It has not been often, or many times, surpassed in the battles of the world. Two hundred and fifty guns, at least, rapidly fired for two mortal hours. Cipher out the number of tons of gunpowder and iron that made these two hours hideous.

At three o'clock almost precisely the last shot hummed, and bounded and fell, and the cannonade was over. Men began to breathe more freely, and to ask, What next, I wonder? There was a pause between acts, with the curtain down, soon to rise upon the great final act, and catastrophe of Gettysburg.

We have passed by the left of the Second Division, coming from the First; when we crossed the crest the enemy was not in sight, and all was still—we walked slowly along in the rear of the troops, by the ridge cut off now from a view of the enemy in his position, and were returning to the spot where we had left our horses. We were near our horses when we noticed Brigadier General [Henry J.] Hunt, Chief of Artillery of the Army, swiftly moving about on horseback, and apparently in a rapid manner giving some orders about the guns. Thought we, what could this mean? In a moment afterwards we met Captain Wessels and the orderlies who had our horses; they were on foot leading the horses. Captain Wessels was pale, and he said, excited: "General, they say the enemy's infantry is advancing." We sprang into our saddles, a score of bounds brought us upon the all-seeing crest.

None on that crest now need be told that *the*

Major General Winfield Scott Hancock, U.S.A.

enemy is advancing. Every eye could see his legions, an overwhelming resistless tide of an ocean of armed men sweeping upon us! Regiment after regiment and brigade after brigade move from the woods and rapidly take their places in the lines forming the assault. More than half a mile their front extends; more than a thousand yards the dull gray masses deploy, man touching man, rank pressing rank, and line supporting line. The red flags wave, their horsemen gallop up and down; the arms of eighteen thousand men, barrel and bayonet, gleam in the sun, a sloping forest of flashing steel.

[*Haskell exaggerates slightly; Pickett had approximately 15,000 men with him when he made his charge.*]

Right on they move, as with one soul, in perfect order, over ridge and slope, through orchard and meadow, and cornfield, magnificent, grim, irresistible.

All was orderly and still upon our crest; no noise and no confusion. General Gibbon rode down the lines, cool and calm, and in an unimpassioned voice he said to the men, "Do not hurry, men, and fire too fast, let them come up close before you fire, and then aim low and steadily." The coolness of their General was reflected in the faces of his men.

Five minutes have elapsed since first the enemy have emerged from the woods. Should these advancing men pierce our line and become the entering wedge, driven home, that would sever our army asunder, what hope would there be afterwards, and where the blood-earned fruits of yesterday? None of these considerations either depressed or elevated us. They might have done the former, had we been timid; the latter had we been confident and vain. But, we were there waiting, and ready to do our duty—that done, results could not dishonor us.

Our skirmishers open a spattering fire along the front, and, fighting, retire upon the main line—the first drops, the heralds of the storm, sounding on our windows. All our available guns are now active, and from the fire of shells, as the range grows shorter and shorter, they change to shrapnel, and from shrapnel to canister; but in spite of shells, and shrapnel and canister, without wavering or halt, the hardy lines of the enemy continue to move on. The Rebel guns make no reply to ours, and no charging shout rings out to-day, as is the Rebel wont; but the courage of these silent men amid our shots seems not to need the stimulus of other noise.

And so across all that broad open ground they have come, nearer and nearer, nearly half the way, with our guns bellowing in their faces, until now a hundred yards, no more, divide our ready left from their advancing right. The eager men there are impatient to begin.

Let them. First, Harrow's breastworks flame; then Hall's; then Webb's. As if our bullets were the fire coals that touched off their muskets, the enemy in front halts, and his countless level barrels blaze back upon us. The Second Division is struggling in battle. The rattling storm soon spreads to the right. All along each hostile front, a thousand yards, with narrowest space between, the volleys blaze and roll; as thick the sound as when a summer hail-storm pelts the city roofs; as thick the fire as when the incessant lightning fringes a summer cloud.

[*The three officers mentioned by Haskell here were the brigade commanders in Gibbon's 2nd Division— Brigadier General William Harrow, Brigadier General Alexander S. Webb, and Colonel Norman J. Hall.*]

When the Rebel infantry had opened fire our batteries soon became silent. The conflict is left to the infantry alone. It was tremendous, but I had seen no wavering in all our line.

Wondering how long the Rebel ranks, deep though they were, could stand our sheltered volleys, I had come near my destination, when—great heaven! were my senses mad? The larger portion of Webb's brigade, by the group of trees and the angles of the wall, was breaking from the cover of their works, and was falling back, a fear-stricken flock of confusion! The fate of Gettysburg hung upon a spider's single thread!

A great magnificent passion came on me at the instant. My sword, that had always hung idle by my side, the sign of rank only in every battle, I drew, bright and gleaming, the symbol of command. All rules and proprieties were forgotten; all considerations of person and danger and safety despised; for, as I met the tide of these rabbits, the red flags of the rebellion began to thicken and flaunt along the wall. I ordered these men to "halt," and "face about" and "fire," and they heard my voice and gathered my meaning, and obeyed my commands. On some unpatriotic backs of those not quick of comprehension, the flat of my sabre fell not lightly, and at its touch their love of country returned, and, with a look at me as if I were the destroying angel, as I might have become theirs, they again faced the enemy.

[Haskell's paragraphs about the supposed rout of Webb's brigade drew down on him, early in the twentieth century, the distilled wrath of the organized survivors of that brigade. Reading his narrative after it had been reprinted by the Wisconsin History Commission, the survivors assembled and passed a series of resolutions upholding the valor of their own brigade and denouncing Haskell as a vainglorious person who had denigrated the bravery of a combat unit in order to magnify his own role as staff officer. The fact seems to be that Webb's brigade was driven away from the stone wall but that nothing like a genuine rout took place. The Confederates did break the Union line at this point, but the break was not large enough for them to exploit properly.]

The men that had fallen back, facing the enemy, soon regained confidence in themselves, and became steady. This portion of the wall was lost to us, and the enemy had gained the cover of the reverse side, where he now stormed with fire. But our men, with their bodies in part protected by the abruptness of the crest, now sent back in the enemies' faces as fierce a storm. Little could be seen of the enemy, by reason of his cover and the smoke, except the flash of his muskets and his waving flags. These red flags were accumulating at the wall every moment, and they maddened us as the same color does the bull.

Webb's men are falling fast, and he is among them to direct and to encourage; but, however well they may now do, with that walled enemy in front, with more than a dozen flags to Webb's three, it soon becomes apparent that in not many minutes they will be overpowered, or that there will be none alive for the enemy to overpower. Webb has but three regiments, all small, the 69th, the 71st and 72d Pennsylvania—the 106th Pennsylvania, except two companies, is not here to-day—and he must have speedy assistance, or this crest will be lost.

Oh, where is Gibbon? where is Hancock?—some general—anybody with the power and the will to support that wasting, melting line? No general came, and no succor! I thought of Hayes upon the right, but from the smoke and war along his front, it was evident that he had enough upon his hands, if he stayed the inrolling tide of the Rebels there. Doubleday upon the

R. Houdon

left was too far off and too slow, and on another occasion I had begged him to send his idle regiments to support another line battling with thrice its numbers, and this "Old Sumpter Hero" had declined. As a last resort I resolved to see if Hall and Harrow could not send some of their commands to reinforce Webb. I galloped to the left in the execution of my purpose, and as I attained the rear of Hall's line, from the nature of the ground and the position of the enemy it was easy to discover the reason and the manner of this gathering of Rebel flags in front of Webb.

[Haskell obviously had a low opinion of Major General Abner Doubleday, who had been a member of the original garrison at Fort Sumter (which Haskell, like many others in that day, consistently misspelled "Sumpter"). His assertion that Doubleday on an earlier occasion had refused to send help may refer to the battle of Antietam, in which Gibbon's brigade was very heavily engaged, with severe losses. In that fight Doubleday had succeeded to the command of the division in which Gibbon's brigade belonged, and Haskell seems to have blamed him for Gibbon's inability to get reinforcements. It might be noted that at Gettysburg, when Reynolds was killed, Doubleday took over command of the First Corps by right of seniority, but that Meade refused to let him retain the command; while the battle was still being fought, Meade detached Major General John Newton from command of a division in the Sixth Corps and sent him over to replace Doubleday at the head of the First Corps. The "Hayes" Haskell mentions was Brigadier General Alexander Hays, commander of the 3rd Division of the Second Corps.]

The enemy, emboldened by his success in gaining our line by the group of trees and the angle of the wall, was concentrating all his right against and was further pressing that point. There was the stress of his assault; there would he drive his fiery wedge to split our line. In front of Harrow's and Hall's Brigades he had been able to advance no nearer than when he first halted to deliver fire, and these commands had not yielded an inch. To effect the concentration before Webb, the enemy would march the regiment on his extreme right of each of his lines by the left flank to the rear of the troops, still halted and facing to the front, and so continuing to draw in his right, when they were all massed in the position desired, he would again face them to the front, and advance to the storming. This was the way he made the wall before Webb's line blaze red with his battle flags, and such was the purpose there of his thick-crowding battalions.

Not a moment must be lost. Colonel Hall I found just in rear of his line, sword in hand, cool, vigilant, noting all that passed and directing the battle of his brigade. "How is it going?" Colonel Hall asked me, as I rode up. "Well, but Webb is hotly pressed and must have support, or he will be overpowered. Can you assist him?" "Yes." "You cannot be too quick."

He gave the order, and in briefest time I saw five friendly colors hurrying to the aid of the imperilled three. The regiments marched by the right flank. Col. Hall superintended the movement in person. The movement was difficult; but in reasonable time, Hall's men are fighting gallantly side by side with Webb's before the all important point. I did not stop to see all this movement of Hall's, but from him I went at once further to the left, to the 1st brigade. Gen'l Harrow I did not see, but his fighting men would answer my purpose as well. All men that I could find I took over to the right at the *double quick.*

As we were moving to, and near the other brigade of the division, from my position on horseback I could see that the enemy's right, under Hall's fire, was beginning to stagger and to break. "See," I said to the men, "see the *chivalry*! See the gray-backs run!" The men saw, and as they swept to their places by the side of Hall and opened fire, they roared, and this in a manner that said more plainly than words—for the deaf could have seen it in their faces, and the blind could have heard it in their voices—*the crest is safe!*

[Pickett's men advanced over a very wide front, but wheeled together as they neared the crest in order to mass numbers in front of the chosen objective—the ground in and around the little group of trees and the angle in the stone wall. A certain part of the Confederate maneuvers here were not so much due to the punishing effect of Union rifle fire as to the tactical necessity for massing men at the decisive point.]

Before the 2nd Division the enemy is massed, the main bulk of his force covered by the ground that slopes to his rear, with his front at the stone wall. Formation of companies and regiments in our ranks is lost; but commands, companies, regiments and brigades are blended and intermixed—an irregular extended mass—men enough, if in order, to form a line of four or five ranks along the whole front of the division. The twelve flags of the regiments wave defiantly at intervals along the front; at the stone wall,

The map on the facing page shows general positions of the two armies on the afternoon of July 3, when Pickett made his famous charge. The previous afternoon's fighting had causd many changes in Federal troop dispositions, and many of the elements of different corps were intermixed. The charge was received by two divisions of the Second Corps.

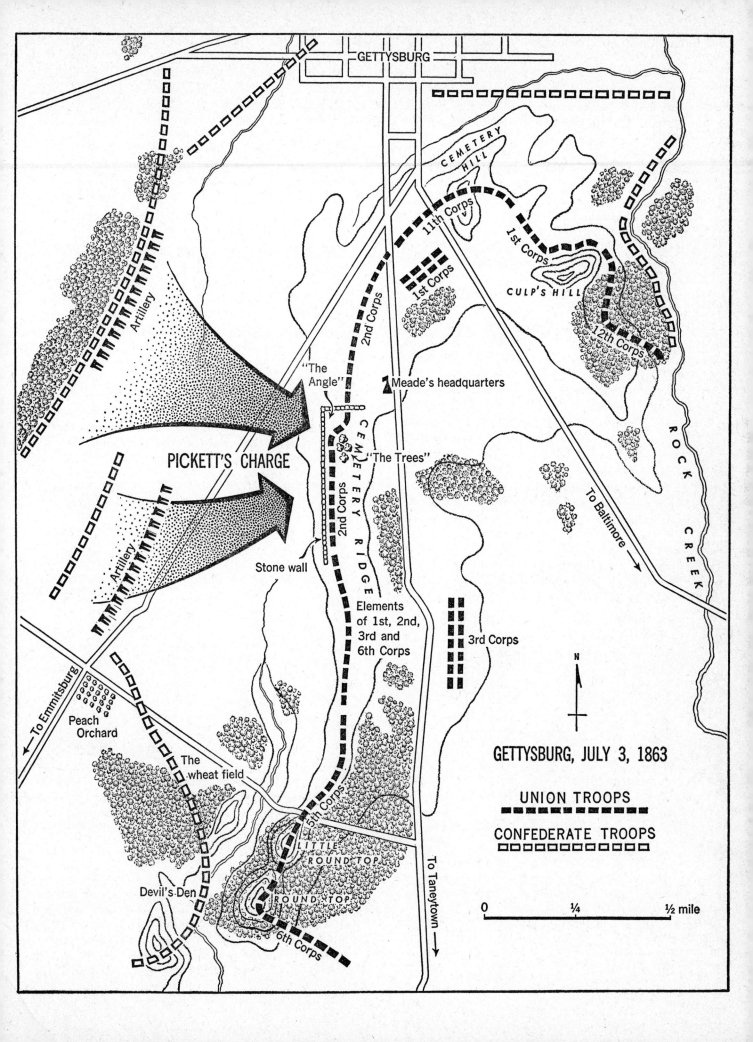

GETTYSBURG

CEMETERY HILL

CULP'S HILL

11th Corps

1st Corps

1st Corps

12th Corps

ROCK CREEK

2nd Corps

1st Corps

"The Angle"

⊾ Meade's headquarters

PICKETT'S CHARGE

Artillery

Artillery

CEMETERY RIDGE

2nd Corps

"The Trees"

To Baltimore →

Stone wall

Elements
of 1st, 2nd,
3rd and
6th Corps

3rd Corps

N

To Emmitsburg →

Peach
Orchard

The
wheat field

5th Corps

LITTLE
ROUND
TOP

ROUND TOP

To Taneytown →

Devil's Den

6th Corps

GETTYSBURG, JULY 3, 1863

UNION TROOPS
■■■■■■■■■■■■■■

CONFEDERATE TROOPS
▯▯▯▯▯▯▯▯▯▯▯▯▯▯

0   ¼   ½ mile

at unequal distances from ours of forty, fifty or sixty yards, stream nearly double this number of the battle flags of the enemy. Now it was as if a new battle, deadlier, stormier than before, had sprung from the body of the old.

The jostling, swaying lines on either side boil and roar and dash their flamy spray, two hostile billows of a fiery ocean. Thick flashes stream from the wall, thick volleys answer from the crest. All depths of passion are stirred, and all combatives fire, down to their deep foundations. Individuality is drowned in a sea of clamor, and timid men, breathing the breath of the multitude, are brave. The men do not cheer or shout; they growl, and over that uneasy sea, heard with the roar of musketry, sweeps the muttered thunder of a storm of growls.

Now the loyal wave rolls up as if it would overleap its barrier, the crest. These men of Pennsylvania, on the soil of their own homesteads, the first and only to flee the wall, must be the first to storm it.

"Major—, *lead* your men over the crest, they will follow." "By the tactics I understand my place is in rear of the men." "Your pardon, sir; I see *your* place is in rear of the men. I thought you were fit to lead." "Sergeant, forward with your color. Let the Rebels see it close to their eyes once before they die."

The color sergeant of the 72d Pennsylvania, grasping the stump of the severed lance in both his hands, waved the flag above his head and rushed towards the wall. One man only starts to follow. Almost half way to the wall, down go color bearer and color to the ground—the gallant sergeant is dead. The line springs —the crest of the solid ground, with a great roar, heaves forward its maddened load, men, arms, smoke, fire, a fighting mass. It rolls to the wall—flash meets flash, the wall is crossed—a moment ensues of thrusts, yells, blows, shots, and undistinguishable conflict, followed by a shout universal that makes the welkin ring again, and the last and bloodiest fight of the great battle of Gettysburg is ended and won.

[*It needs to be borne in mind in this portion of the narrative that the Union line was approximately 100 yards in front of the actual crest of Cemetery Ridge. When Pickett's men broke through, the Union defenders retired to the crest of the ridge and held their ground there, keeping up a sharp fire; eventually they swept down the slope and drove the gallant survivors of Pickett's spearhead out of the ground that had been seized. It should be pointed out that although the Confederates brought up the slope many more men than the Second Union Corps had for defense, their troops were actually outnumbered at the actual point of penetration. Once the Unionists were rallied for a counterattack, Pickett's case was hopeless.*]

Many things cannot be described by pen or pencil —such a fight is one. Some hints and incidents may be given, but a description or picture never. From what

is told the imagination may for itself construct the scene; otherwise he who never saw can have no adequate idea of what such a battle is.

When the vortex of battle passion had subsided, hopes, fears, rage, joy, of which the maddest and the noisiest was the last, and we were calm enough to look about us, we saw that, as with us, the fight with the Third Division was ended, and that in that division was a repetition of the scenes immediately about us. In that moment the judgment almost refused to credit the senses. Are these abject wretches about us, whom our men are now disarming and driving together in flocks, the jaunty men of Pickett's Division, whose steady lines and flashing arms but a few moment's since came sweeping up the slope to destroy us? Are these red cloths that our men toss about in derision the "fiery Southern crosses," thrice ardent, the battle flags of the rebellion that waved defiance at the wall? We know, but so sudden has been the transition, we yet can scarce believe.

Just as the fight was over, and the first outburst of victory had a little subsided, when all in front of the crest was noise and confusion—prisoners being collected, small parties in pursuit of them far down into the fields, flags waving, officers giving quick, sharp commands to their men—I stood apart for a few moments upon the crest, by that group of trees which ought to be historic forever, a spectator of the thrilling scene around. Some few musket shots were still heard in the Third Division; and the enemy's guns, almost silent since the advance of his infantry until the moment of his defeat, were dropping a few sullen shells among friend and foe upon the crest.

It is not an hour since these legions were sweeping along so grandly; now sixteen hundred of that fiery mass are strewn among the trampled grass, dead as the clods. More than seven thousand, probably eight thousand, are wounded, among them Generals Pettigrew, Garnett, Kemper and Armistead, the last three mortally, and the last one in our hands. "Tell General Hancock," he said to Lieutenant Mitchell, Hancock's aide-de-camp, to whom he handed his watch,

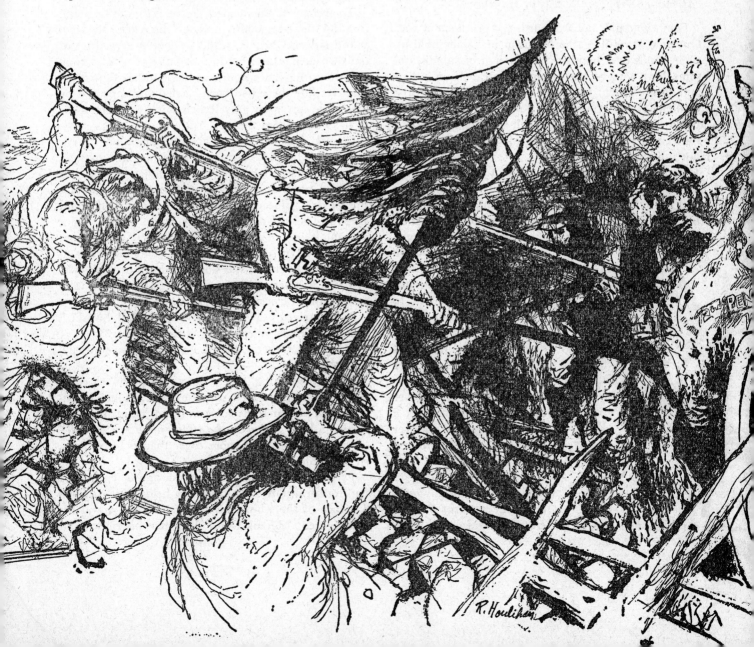

"that I know I did my country a great wrong when I took up arms against her, for which I am sorry, but for which I cannot live to atone."

[Brigadier General Lewis A. Armistead, commanding a brigade in Pickett's division, had been a close friend of Hancock before the war, and the two had exchanged emotional good-byes at a farewell party in an army post in California in the spring of 1861, when Armistead and other Southern officers resigned their commissions in order to come east and serve with the Confederacy. Armistead died among Cushing's guns at the point where Pickett's men briefly broke the Union line, and his last thought apparently was of Hancock.]

Four thousand, not wounded, are prisoners of war. Our men are still "gathering them in." Some hold up their hands or a handkerchief in sign of submission; some have hugged the ground to escape our bullets and so are taken; few made resistance after the first moment of our crossing the wall; some yield submissively with good grace, some with grim, dogged aspect, showing that but for the other alternative they could not submit to this.

Such was really the closing scene of the grand drama of Gettysburg. After repeated assaults upon the right and the left, where, and in all of which repulse had been his only success, this persistent and presuming enemy forms his chosen troops, the flower of his army, for a grand assault upon our center. The manner and result of such assault have been told—a loss to the enemy of from twelve thousand to fourteen thousand, killed, wounded and prisoners, and of over thirty battle-flags. This was accomplished by not over six thousand men, with a loss on our part of not over two thousand five hundred killed and wounded.

[Haskell substantially overstates the total of Confederate losses in this fight. The three Confederate divisions involved in the attack had total casualties of approximately 7,600 men at Gettysburg. Two of these divisions had incurred a good part of these losses in the fighting on the first day; and the over-all losses in the charge on July 3 were undoubtedly much nearer 5,000 than the 12,000 to 14,000 mentioned by Haskell. Pickett's own division, of course—numbering about one-third of the total in the assaulting column—was practically wrecked by its losses.]

Would to Heaven General Hancock and Gibbon could have stood there where I did, and have looked upon that field! It would have done two men, to whom the country owes much, good to have been with their men in that moment of victory. But they are both severely wounded and have been carried from the field. One person did come then that I was glad to see there, and that was no less than Major General Meade, whom the Army of the Potomac was fortunate enough to have at that time to command it.

To appreciate the incident I give, it should be borne in mind that one coming up from the rear of the line, as did General Meade, could have seen very little of our own men. One who did not know results, so coming, would have been quite as likely to have supposed that our line there had been carried and captured by the enemy—so many gray Rebels were on the crest—as to have discovered the real truth.

General Meade rode up, accompanied alone by his son, who is his aide-de-camp. The principal horseman was no bedizened hero of some holiday review, but he was a plain man, dressed in a serviceable summer suit of dark blue cloth, without badge or ornament, save the shoulder-straps of his grade, and a light, straight sword of a General or General staff officer. He wore heavy, high-top boots and buff gauntlets, and his soft black felt hat was slouched down over his eyes. His face was very white, not pale, and the lines were marked and earnest and full of care.

As he arrived near me, coming up the hill, he asked, in a sharp, eager voice: "How is it going here?"

"I believe, General, the enemy's attack is repulsed," I answered.

Still approaching, and a new light began to come in his face, of gratified surprise, with a touch of incredulity, of which his voice was also the medium, he further asked: *"What! Is the assault already repulsed?"* his voice quicker and more eager than before. "It is, sir," I replied.

By this time he was on the crest, and when his eye had for an instant swept over the field, taking in just a glance of the whole, he said, impressively, and his face lighted: "Thank God." And then his right hand moved as if it would have caught off his hat and waved it; but this gesture he suppressed, and instead he waved his hand, and said "Hurrah!" The son, with more youth in his blood and less rank upon his shoulders, snatched off his cap, and roared out his three "hurrahs" right heartily. The General then surveyed the field, some minutes, in silence. He at length asked who was in command—he had heard that Hancock and Gibbon were wounded—and I told him that General Caldwell was the senior officer of the Corps and General Harrow of the Division.

He asked where they were, but before I had time to answer that I did not know, he resumed: "No matter, I will give my orders to you and you will see them executed." He then gave direction that the troops should be reformed as soon as practicable, and kept in their places, as the enemy might be mad enough to attack again. He also gave directions concerning the posting of some reinforcements which he said should soon be there, adding: "If the enemy does attack, charge him in the flank and sweep him from the field; do you understand." The General then, a gratified man, galloped in the direction of his headquarters.

[*Haskell's description of his meeting with Meade drew the sarcasm of the survivors of Webb's brigade when they read his story in 1909. In a pamphlet which they published the survivors referred scornfully to Haskell as "this Wellington of Lee's Waterloo," and suggested that Meade would hardly have left all arrangements for a counterattack in the hands of a mere first lieutenant. Since Meade's army made no gesture toward such an attack the point hardly seems to be of great importance.*]

Then the work of the field went on. First, the prisoners were collected and sent to the rear. "There go the men," the Rebels were heard to say, by some of our surgeons who were in Gettysburg, at the time Pickett's Division marched out to take position— "There go the men that will go through your d——d Yankee lines, for you." A good many of them did "go through our lines for us," but in a very different way from the one they intended—not impetuous victors, sweeping away our thin lines with ball and bayonet, but crestfallen captives, without arms, with the cheers of their conquerors ringing in their ears. There was a grim truth after all in this Rebel remark.

In view of the results of that day—the successes of the arms of the country—would not the people of the whole country, standing there upon the crest with General Meade, have said, with him: "Thank God?"

I have no knowledge and little notion of how long a time elapsed from the moment the fire of the infantry commenced, until the enemy was entirely re-

pulsed, in this his grand assault. I judge, from the amount of fighting and the changes of position that occurred, that probably the fight was of nearly an hour's duration, but I cannot tell, and I have seen none who knew. The time seemed but a very few minutes, when the battle was over.

When the prisoners were cleared away and order was again established upon our crest, where the conflict

Brigadier General Lewis Addison Armistead, C.S.A.

had impaired it, until between five and six o'clock, I remained upon the field, directing some troops to their position, in conformity to the orders of General Meade. Of the pursuit of the enemy and the movements of the army subsequent to the battle, until the crossing of the Potomac by Lee and the closing of the campaign, it is not my purpose to write. Suffice it that on the night of the 3d of July the enemy withdrew his left from our front, and on the morning of the 4th we again occupied the village of Gettysburg, and on that national day victory was proclaimed to the country; that floods of rain on that day prevented army movements of any considerable magnitude, the day being passed by our army in position upon the field, in burying our dead, and some of those of the enemy, and in making the movements already indicated; that on the 5th the pursuit of the enemy was commenced— his dead were buried by us—and the corps of our army, upon various roads, moved from the battlefield.

With a statement of some of the results of the battle, as to losses and captures, and of what I saw in riding over the field, when the enemy was gone, my account is done.

The magnitude of the armies engaged, the number of the casualties, the object sought by the Rebel, the result, will all contribute to give Gettysburg a place among the great historic battles of the world. That General Meade's concentration was rapid—over thirty miles a day was marched by some of the Corps—that his position

Major General George Edward Pickett, C.S.A.

was skillfully selected and his dispositions good; that he fought the battle hard and well; that his victory was brilliant and complete, I think all should admit. I cannot but regard it as highly fortunate to us and commendable in General Meade, that the enemy was allowed the initiative, the offensive, in the main battle; that it was much better to allow the Rebel, for his own destruction, to come up and smash his lines and columns upon the defensive solidity of our position, than it would have been to hunt him, for the same purpose, in the woods, or to unearth him from his rifle-pits. In this manner our losses were lighter, and his heavier, than if the case had been reversed. And whatever the books may say of troops fighting the better who make the attack, I am satisfied that in this war, Americans, the Rebels as well as ourselves, are best on the defensive.

[Haskell's remark that both Federals and Confederates "are best on the defensive" simply highlights the fact that Civil War weapons had been improved much more than infantry tactics. The rifled infantry musket, muzzle-loader though it was, had vastly increased defensive fire power. The old smooth-bore, on which infantry tactics were still based, was very inaccurate, and was so limited in range that it was ineffective at any distance greater than about 150 yards. The rifle used by Civil War troops could begin to kill at half a mile or more, and the advance in the massed formation—still standard, by the old tactics—was simply out of date. A straight frontal assault against good troops in a properly chosen defensive position had very little chance to succeed, by the 1860's: a lesson that was impressed on the Unionists at Fredericksburg, on Lee at Gettysburg, and on U. S. Grant at the battle of Cold Harbor.]

But men there are who think that nothing was gained or done well in this battle, because some other general did not have the command, or because any portion of the army of the enemy was permitted to escape capture or destruction. It should be enough, perhaps, to say that men who have knowledge enough of military affairs to entitle them to express an opinion on such matters will be most likely to vindicate the Pennsylvania campaign of Gen. Meade, and to see that he accomplished all that could have been reasonably expected of any general of any army. Complaint has been, and is, made specially against Meade, that he did not attack Lee before he had time to withdraw across the river. These were the facts concerning this matter:

The 13th of July was the earliest day when such an attack, if practicable at all, could have been made. The time before this, since the battle, had been spent in moving the army from the vicinity of the field, finding something of the enemy and concentrating before him. On that day the army was concentrated and in order of battle near the turnpike that leads from Sharpesburg to Hagerstown, Md. The mean distance to the Potomac was some six miles, and the enemy was between Meade and the river.

The Potomac, swelled by the recent rain, was boiling and swift and deep, a magnificent place to have drowned all the Rebel crew. I have not the least doubt but that Gen. Meade would have liked to drown them all, if he could, but they were unwilling to be drowned, and would fight first. To drive them into the river then, they must be routed. Gen. Meade, I believe, favored an attack upon the enemy at that time, but at daylight on the morning of the 14th, strong reconnaissances showed that between the enemy, except a thousand or fifteen hundred of his rear guard, who fell into our hands, and the Army of the Potomac, rolled the rapid unbridged river. The enemy had constructed bridges, had crossed during all the preceding night, but so close were our cavalry and infantry upon him in the morning, that the bridges were destroyed before his rear guard had all crossed.

Among the considerations against the propriety of attack at that time were the following: The army was wearied and worn down by four weeks of constant forced marching or battle. What such weariness means few save soldiers know. Since the battle the army had been constantly diminished by sickness or prostration and by more straggling than I ever saw before. The men were near the point when further efficient physical exertion was quite impossible.

The enemy was in position in a ridgy, wooded country, abounding in strong defensive positions, his main bodies concealed, protected by rifle-pits and epaulements, acting strictly on the defensive. To have had a battle there then, Gen. Meade would have had

to attack a cunning enemy in the dark, where surprises, undiscovered rifle-pits and batteries, and unseen bodies of men might have met his forces at every point.

I felt the probability of defeat strongly at the time. I believe the Army of the Potomac is always willing, often eager, to fight the enemy, whenever, as it thinks, there is a fair chance for victory; that it always will fight, let come victory or defeat whenever it is ordered so to do. Of course the army, both officers and men, had very great disappointment and very great sorrow that the Rebels *escaped*—so it was called—across the river; the disappointment was genuine, at least to the extent that disappointment is like surprise; but the sorrow to judge by looks, tones and actions, rather than by words, was not of that deep, sable character for which there is no balm.

[*Abraham Lincoln was one who felt that Meade should not have permitted Lee to get his army back across the Potomac into Virginia, and he expressed himself in a rather bitter letter which he wrote, in the White House—and then decided not to send. It may be worth noting that in the summer of 1957 President Dwight D. Eisenhower and Field Marshal Viscount Montgomery, sauntering about the field at Gettysburg, came to much the same conclusion Lincoln had reached: that Lee should not have been allowed to get his beaten army back to safety. At the same time it should be remembered that Lincoln did not actually send Meade his letter of criticism, and that he retained Meade in command of the Army of the Potomac to the end of the war.*]

. . . At about six o'clock on the afternoon of the 3d of July, my duties done upon the field, I quitted it to go to the General. My brave horse *Dick* was a sight to see. He was literally covered with blood. Struck repeatedly, his right thigh had been ripped

open in a ghastly manner by a piece of shell, and three bullets were lodged deep in his body. Dick's was no mean part in that battle. Most horses would have been unmanageable with the flash and roar of arms about and the shouting. Dick was utterly cool, and would have obeyed the rein had it been a straw. To Dick belongs the honor of first mounting that stormy crest before the enemy, not forty yards away, whose bullets smote him, and of being the only horse there during the heat of the battle. Even the enemy noticed Dick, and one of their reports of the battle mentions the *"solitary horseman"* who rallied our wavering line.

He enabled me to do twelve times as much as I could have done on foot. It would not be dignified for an officer on foot to run; it is entirely so, mounted, to gallop. I do not approve of officers dismounting in battle, which is the time of all when they most need to be mounted, for thereby they have so much greater facilities for being everywhere present.

If there be, *"ut sapientibus placit,"* an equine elysium, I will send to Charon the brass coin, the fee for Dick's passage over, and on the other side of the Styx in those shadowy clover-fields he may nibble the blossoms forever.

On the 6th of July, while my bullet bruise was yet too inflamed and sensitive for me to be good for much in the way of duty—the division was then halted for the day some four miles from the field on the Baltimore turnpike—I could not repress the desire or omit the opportunity to see again where the battle had been. With the right stirrup strap shortened in a manner to favor the bruised leg, I could ride my horse at a walk without serious discomfort. It seemed very strange upon approaching the horse-shoe crest again, not to see it covered with the thousands of troops and horses and guns, but they were all gone—the armies,

to my seeming, had vanished—and on that lovely summer morning the stillness and silence of death pervaded the localities where so recently the shouts and the cannon had thundered.

The recent rains had washed out many an unsightly spot, and smoothed many a harrowed trace of the conflict; but one still needed no guide save the eyes, to follow the track of that storm, which the storms of heaven were powerless soon to entirely efface. The spade and shovel, so far as a little earth for the human bodies would render their task done, had completed their work. The scattered small arms and the accoutrements had been collected and carried away, almost all that were of any value; but great numbers of bent and splintered muskets, rent knapsacks and haversacks, bruised canteens, shreds of caps, coats, trowsers, of blue or gray cloth, worthless belts and cartridge boxes, torn blankets, ammunition boxes, broken wheels, smashed limbers, shattered gun carriages, parts of harness, of all that men or horses wear or use in battle, were scattered broadcast over miles of the field.

Never elsewhere upon any field have I seen such abundant evidences of a terrific fire of cannon and musketry as upon this. Along the enemy's position, where our shells and shot had struck during the cannonade of the third, the trees had cast their trunks and branches as if they had been icicles shaken by a blast. And graves of the Rebel's making, and dead horses and scattered accoutrements, showed that other things besides trees had been struck by our projectiles.

All was bustle and noise in the little town of Gettysburg as I entered it on my tour of the field. From the afternoon of the 1st to the morning of the 4th of July, the enemy was in possession. Very many of the inhabitants had, upon the first approach of the enemy, or upon the retirement of our troops, fled their homes and the town, not to return until after the battle. Now the town was a hospital where gray and blue mingled in about equal proportion.

The public buildings, the courthouse, the churches and many private dwellings were full of wounded. There had been in some of the streets a good deal of fighting, and bullets had thickly spattered the fences and walls, and shells had riddled the houses from side to side. But the people, the women and children that had fled, were returning, or had returned to their homes—such homes—and amid the general havoc were restoring as they could order to the desecrated firesides.

I rode through the Cemetery on "Cemetery Hill." How these quiet sleepers must have been astounded in their graves when the twenty pound Parrott guns thundered above them and the solid shot crushed their gravestones! The flowers, roses and creeping vines that pious hands had planted to bloom and shed their odors over the ashes of the dead ones gone, were trampled upon the ground and black with the cannon's soot. A dead horse lay by the marble shaft, and over it the marble finger pointed to the sky. The marble lamb that had slept its white sleep on the grave of a child, now lies blackened upon a broken gun-carriage. Such are the incongruities and jumblings of battle.

I looked away to *the group of trees*—the Rebel gunners know what ones I mean, and so do the survivors of Pickett's division—and a strange fascination led me thither. How thick are the marks of battle as I approach—the graves of the men of the 3d division of the 2d corps; the splintered oaks, the scattered horses —seventy-one dead horses were on a spot some fifty yards square.

I stood solitary upon the crest by *"the trees"* where, less than three days ago, I had stood before; but now how changed is all the eye beholds. Do these thick mounds cover the fiery hearts that in the battle rage swept the crest and stormed the wall? I read their names—them, alas, I do not know—but I see the regiments marked on their frail monuments—"20th Mass. Vols.," "69 P. V.," "1st Minn. Vols.," and the rest— they are all represented, and as they fought commingled here. So I am not alone. These, my brethren of the fight, are with me. Sleep, noble brave! The foe shall not desecrate your sleep. Yonder thick trenches will hold them. As long as patriotism is a virtue, your deeds have made this crest, your resting place, hallowed ground!

GETTYSBURG TODAY

Where Gallant

Spirits Still

Tell Their Story

In an open field near McPherson's Wood, in a picture made just after the battle, dead men of the 24th Michigan, of the Iron Brigade, testify to the fighting of the first day.

It all happened 94 years ago, and all of the men who were there are dead now; but the ground today is just the same, the sun still slants down in late afternoon from the crest of the blue mountain wall to the west, and quaint, archaic statues mark the places where living men once stormed and shouted at one another . . . and, taking everything together, Gettysburg today is a place where gallant spirits still tell their story of high sacrifice and undying devotion. There is a cemetery, there are gentle ridges rolling unbroken toward the sunset, and here and there one can find spots where everything that is significant in the American dream speaks to today's world with an undying voice.

You can visit Gettysburg now and follow paved roads, between neat stretches of lawn and woodland, with a great number of monuments marking the way, and if there are ghosts there they are very harmless— young Americans, dead nearly a century, whose presence is always felt but who are never in the least frightening. Across the wheat fields (there is *the* wheat field, where several thousand men died in an hour's fight, and there are lesser fields of wheat, very quiet now on land where the casualty lists were somewhat smaller), and peach orchards, and tangled hillocks of rock and scrubby trees, and burly hillsides covered with maples and beeches—across these the visitor can go without once hearing the terrible clamor of battle. Yet the battle was here and its presence is felt, and you

The lawn is green and smooth, and the white headstones are ranked in neat military formation: this is a modern view of part of Gettysburg's military cemetery, with a three-inch iron rifle placed where a battery once spoke for the Union.

JACK LEHART, FPG

49

A dark shadow against dying sunlight, this soldier's statue (left) on East Cemetery Hill marks the place where men of the Second Corps stopped a Confederate attack, on the evening of July 2, which nearly broke the Union line.

cannot visit the place without feeling the echoes of what was once a proving ground for everything America believes in.

For Gettysburg was where we Americans came to grips with ourselves. On these Pennsylvania hills, fate once asked men of our flesh: Do you really mean it? Are you just coasting, or is the vision this land gave you something you are willing to die for? They died on these hills and fields in fantastic numbers, and the dying was not easy, but young men who would have preferred to live did die and this open, sunlit country remembers them, Northerners and Southerners alike.

We are a young country with the future still ahead of us, but we do have our shrines and Gettysburg is one of the greatest of them. It is great because it once brought us face to face with certain fundamentals. These still live with us; we passed one test, and by the story which the passing of that test tells us, we do not need to be afraid of anything that can happen in the future. The America of today was beaten into form on what are now the quiet, dreamy fields around this hilltop town in Pennsylvania.   *—Bruce Catton*

Behind a stone wall on the edge of a quiet wood, these English-made Whitworth rifles peer out today just as they did in 1863, when they helped pave the way for the great assault. Below, wheat grows on the field Pickett's men crossed on their way to the Union-defended ridge.

Man of bronze on a brazen horse: the statue of Robert E. Lee looks out across the field where the Confederacy's greatest attack failed. A 12-pounder (foreground) marks a Southern gun position.

Bonnet,

Weapon in hand and

Biblical imprecations on her lips,

Carry Nation campaigned

to save men

from

the drunkard's fate

By STEWART H. HOLBROOK

Book, and Hatchet

She was born Carry Amelia Moore in Kentucky, in 1846. By the time she came into the public eye she was Carry A. Nation, an amazon nearly six feet tall who kept her weight down to 175 pounds by the prodigious wrecking of saloons. The odd spelling of her first name was due to the imperfect learning of her father. Her mother lived for many years in the delusion that she was Queen Victoria and died in the Missouri State Hospital for the Insane.

In 1867 Carry met and married a young physician, Dr. Charles Gloyd, who showed up at the altar smelling of cloves and alcohol. Marriage did not perform a miracle. In less than two years he was lowered into a drunkard's grave. Ten years later Carry married David Nation, and together they faced a quarter of a century of bickering, battles, and wandering, while the incompetent Nation almost but never quite made a living with his combined talents as a lawyer, an editor, and a minister of the Gospel.

Meantime Mrs. Nation brooded on her troubles, and she concluded, finally, that she had been chosen to become a martyr to a number of causes which included not only temperance but also the abolition of tobacco and all fraternal orders. (Carry's first husband had done a good deal of drinking in the quarters of his lodge, from which women were excluded.) This was the mental baggage she was carrying when the Nations moved again, this time to Medicine Lodge, Kansas, where her husband, in the character of the Reverend David Nation, preached a while before reverting to law; and Mrs. Nation was elected president of the Barber County chapter of the Woman's Christian Temperance Union.

It was an office that she accepted with the utmost seriousness. Kansas was technically dry by constitutional amendment, but actually pretty wet because of the profound appetites of the farmers for the end product of their handsome fields of corn, wheat, and rye. Medicine Lodge alone, as Mrs. Nation quickly discovered, supported seven drinking places, or "joints," as saloons were popularly known throughout Kansas. She set about to close them by writing appeals to the governor and the attorney general of the state, to the sheriff of Barber County, and to various newspapers. None so much as replied. In this extremity, as she related in her autobiography, Carry Nation had recourse to prayer and divination; and on the afternoon of June 5, 1900, with her eyes tightly shut, she jabbed a pin at random into her opened Bible, then looked to see that she had impaled the sixtieth chapter of Isaiah: "Arise, shine; for thy light is come, and the glory of the Lord is risen upon thee."

Carry was ready to rise and shine, and within a few minutes "a musical voice murmured in her ear" a command to go to Kiowa—a town reputed to be the wettest in Barber County. Presently the voice added: "Take something in your hands and throw at those places and smash them!" Only then did she know exactly what she was to do.

Next day at dawn she bounced out of bed in exaltation. Singing snatches of hymns, she went into the back yard to assemble a creditable pile of stones and bricks. She wrapped these one by one in old newspapers, put them into the buggy, hitched up her horse, and drove out of Medicine Lodge on the jolting and dusty road to Kiowa, nigh twenty miles distant, and destiny. Having arrived after nightfall, she lay low till morning, then hitched up her rig and drove to the joint operated by a Mr. Dobson, there to make history.

With a dozen or more of the missiles stacked upon her left arm, she pushed open the saloon door to find a few hung-over men working hopefully on their eye openers. They stared incredibly at the apparition of this motherly woman (Carry was 54 years old) in a whisky joint, but they stared only briefly. "Men," said she, "I have come to save you from a drunkard's fate!" Then she let go with her neolithic artillery.

She had a powerful arm and, unlike most women, she could throw. Her first missile smashed the large mirror behind the bar. The second was a perfect strike that shattered every glass on the back bar and also broke several bottles. Now sure of herself, she poured a torrent of paper-wrapped stones at the surviving bottles of liquor, then turned to address the poor proprietor.

"Now, Mr. Dobson," she said, "I have finished. God be with you." She flounced out of the devastated joint, got into her buggy, and was about to drive off when a happy idea took her. Reaching under the seat, she picked up two more of her neatly packaged stones and heaved them through Mr. Dobson's windows. Then she set her horse to walking briskly down the street.

Kiowa's horrible day was not done, for Carry's ammunition was no more exhausted than she. In a matter of minutes she made desolation of two more joints, improving her original technique by ripping several prints of actresses and sporting figures from the walls, overturning beer tables, smashing chairs, to emerge from the last joint smelling gloriously of the alcohol sprayed by breaking bottles and running in riverlets over the barroom floor. She made no haste to leave the stricken town, but courted the attention of the city marshal and the mayor, of whom she demanded to be arrested. The officials declined, and

"I CANNOT TELL A LIE—I DID IT WITH MY LITTLE HATCHET!"
Mrs. Nation's Reform Crusade in Kansas, as the Globe Artist Understands It From the Press Skirmishes.

In a 1901 cartoon from the Utica Globe, *a militant Carry Nation menaces a terrified Kansas barkeep. "Saloon property," she said, "has no rights that anybody is bound to respect."*

Carry Nation drove out of Kiowa in what until then was the incomparable triumph of her life.

The Kiowa raid was given only short notice in Wichita and Topeka papers, but more, much more, was to come. Carry Nation was resolved to lay waste to every joint in the state, including what she called "the murder mills of the metropolis of Wichita."

Wichita was as wet as a bar rag. Forty-odd joints ran openly with no concealment other than curtained windows and doors. Each displayed a modest sign, "Sample Room," the current cryptogram for saloon, especially in dry territory. A few more were operated in conjunction with eating places. Another reason Wichita attracted Mrs. Nation was that a majority of Kansas wholesale liquor dealers had their warehouses there.

For her first sortie into Wichita, Carry Nation dressed in the garb she wore to the end of her career: a black alpaca dress fastened by a row of dark pearl buttons extending up the left side from hem to yoke; a broad bow of white ribbon at her throat; heavy, square-toed shoes; black cotton stockings; a black poke bonnet with a silk ribbon tied under her chin; and, except in hot weather, a heavy cape of navy blue cloth. Almost always she carried an umbrella. Cartoonists, with whom she was for many years a favorite character, found her getup perfect for quick and easy delineation.

She was thus attired when she took a train of steamcars for Wichita, save that in place of the umbrella she carried her husband's rugged walking stick and a valise in which she had put a foot-long iron rod. The press of Wichita had not been warned of her coming. On her first day in the city she went forth to inspect the sample rooms and made no comment until she entered the most elegant joint in all Kansas. This was operated in the basement of the Hotel Carey, and its long, curved bar reflected the brilliance of hundreds of electric lights. On one wall her beady black eyes did not miss an enormous oil painting, *Cleopatra at the Bath.* She stopped dead in her tracks.

Carry Nation had not planned to pass any comment during this her initial tour of Wichita joints, but the naked Cleopatra changed her mind. She reflected—so she wrote later—that woman is stripped of everything by the saloons. Her husband is torn from her. She is robbed of her sons. Then they take away her clothes "and her virtue." This reflection occupied Mrs. Nation no more than a moment. She strode to the bar, pointed a quivering finger at the startled bartender.

"Young man," she demanded, "what are you doing in this hellhole?"

"I'm sorry, madam," he replied, "but we do not serve ladies."

"Serve *me?*" screamed Carry Nation. "Do you think I'd drink your hellish poison?" She pointed at Cleopatra. "Take that filthy thing down," she cried, "and close this murder-mill."

Then she snatched a bottle from the bar, threw it to the floor, and ran out into the street. She returned to her hotel, to muse on the Hotel Carey bar, "this hell glittering with crystallized tears," and to take from her valise the short iron bar. This she bound with stout cord to the cane and, hiding this formidable weapon beneath her cape, returned in the morning to the Hotel Carey, pausing in an alley to pick up a fair load of stones, which she wrapped in a newspaper. Now she was ready for Cleopatra.

On cat's feet the enemy of Cleopatra entered the Carey bar to find bartender Parker serving half a dozen men. They had time only to gape before Carry started heaving rocks that smashed the immense gilt frame and tore through the canvas. "Glory to God!"

she shouted. "Peace on earth, good will to men!" Then she heaved another stone to crash almost into the exact center of the great mirror behind the bar. ("Cost fifteen hunnert dollars," bartender Parker told the police.) It tumbled in fragments.

The drinkers and bartender lammed through the rear doorway, and Carry moved into the second phase of the battle. Bringing forth the wicked tool she had fashioned from cane and iron rod, she tore around one end of the bar and began slashing at the orderly array of bottles, decanters, and glassware on the back bar. All disintegrated with a most satisfying noise. When Detective Park Massey, followed by curious guests, walked into the saloon, Carry had lifted one of the finest and biggest brass cuspidors in Kansas to the top of the cherry bar and was beating it furiously.

"Madam," said the officer, "I must arrest you for defacing property."

"Defacing?" she screamed. "Defacing? I am defacing nothing! I am *destroying!*"

The general appearance of the Hotel Carey bar indicated Mrs. Nation had a better understanding of the niceties of the language than did Detective Massey. When she was taken before Judge O. D. Kirk, the charge was read and Mrs. Nation was asked whether she pled guilty. "I'll have nothing to do with this court," she snapped, "until that man over there throws away his cigar. It's rotten and the smell of it poisons me." And "that man," who happened to be the prosecuting attorney, dropped the offending cigar into a cuspidor.

There was a terrible to-do about Carry Nation in the Kansas courts before she was released on bail, and at last the charges were dismissed because, said the prosecuting attorney, he feared for the crusader's mental condition. The crusader's mental condition was unchanged, or perhaps it was intensified, by the hundreds of congratulatory telegrams, letters, and callers that flooded her. There were many requests for help from women in towns and cities all over Kansas and from other states. Carry Nation was delighted. She felt she was on the way to the martyrdom and fame she strongly wanted. Even New York City and Boston papers had given front-page notice of her destruction of the Hotel Carey's saloon.

There is no need to tell of more than one of the score or more subsequent raids, all during 1901, which by year's end had made her incomparably the most notorious female character in the United States. The raid in question gave her the symbol by which she is best remembered half a century later. It also shows graphically the perfection of technique she had achieved. This attack was in Topeka, to which Carry had

come in order "to free the Capital of Kansas from the shame of its saloons." With her she brought four brand-new hatchets that cost 85 cents each and were of the same fine quality as one she had used with terrible effect on the Douglas Avenue Sample Room of James Burnes, in Wichita.

Snow was falling heavily in Topeka when, at the ungodly hour of six in the morning, Mrs. Nation, a Mrs. John White, and a Miss Madeline Southard, a local evangelist of some power, met on Kansas Avenue and proceeded to the restaurant (and barroom) of E. C. Russam, who had got word that the now-famous enemy of whisky was in town. At the entrance of his

In jail for one of her bar-smashing escapades, Carry kneels with her Bible. Arrested about thirty times, she paid her fines from lecture fees and the sale of souvenir hatchets.

place, even at this early hour, the three women ran head-on into a couple of surly guards and were defeated after a brisk contact during which Mrs. Nation sustained slight wounds from her own weapon on forehead and one hand.

Pausing only long enough to stanch the flow of blood with handkerchiefs, the three raiders plodded through the deepening snow across Kansas Avenue, to note there were no guards on duty at the elegant entrance to the Senate Bar, Topeka's finest drinking establishment. Mrs. Nation, Mrs. White, and Miss Southard pushed open the door and entered without disturbing Benner Tucker, the popular and efficient bartender, who was busy polishing glasses. He became aware of his visitors when he heard pounding and the tinkle of breaking glass.

Mr. Tucker turned instantly to see Miss Southard at work with bright shining hatchet on the cigar case,

CONTINUED ON PAGE 120

The pride of early locomotive builders is evidenced in their fine lithographs. This one shows a classic "American" type wo

FAREWELL TO STEAM

The iron horses that built America are nearly all gathered on the other side of Jordan

By OLIVER JENSEN

rner, built in 1856 by the Amoskeag Manufacturing Company of Manchester, N.H. Behind are the great Amoskeag textile mills.

It was the way they worked the cord and changed the steam pressure that made the whistle almost seem to talk. Of course, there was a regular language of signals—two long blasts for starting up; one long tremolo for approaching a station; and, at grade crossings, the familiar *whoooo, whoooo, hoo, whoooooooooo!* mournful and infinitely expressive—but within these supposed rigidities there was plenty of room for individuality. An engineer was a man of importance, admired by young and old, and the whistle was his signature. It was the notes of a whippoorwill, they say, that signified to the Mississippi field

The railway itself was devised before any engine was perfected to run on it. The oxen at right were still hauling freight wagons on the yard track of the Lazell, Perkins iron works at Bridgewater, Massachusetts, in 1860, but steam pulled the cars of the Fall River Railroad. Below is a sail car on the South Carolina Railroad, later the scene of the first regular train service behind a steam engine. This line also had the first fatality, when the fireman sat on the safety valve and was boosted to glory by the immutable laws of physics.

CULVER SERVICE

hands that Casey Jones was roaring by in his fast ten-wheeler, No. 382. But down in the cornfield, alas, you no longer hear that mournful sound, for not only Casey but also most of the steam locomotives in America have gone to the Promised Land, and all there is to hear is the blast of the diesel air horn.

We have grown accustomed in our times to the ever-accelerating tempo of social and economic change; even so, the whistle of the steam engine seems to have fallen silent with stunning speed. Steam was still king at the end of World War II and had reigned supreme for over one hundred years. Like the dinosaur on the verge of extinction, it had swollen to enormous size, a hard-breathing, towering monster. Yet its hour has struck so suddenly that it seems quite possible that

many a child is being born who will never see a steam locomotive, except as a toy or curio.

If the child lives in a city, especially an eastern city like New York or Boston, his chances are pretty slim. The last steam engine on the New York Central, No. 1977, chuffed her last in May, and there has not been a single New England carrier trailing smoke since the Central Vermont damped its fires in the spring. The smoke pall which so recently filled the train sheds of Boston and dirtied alike the linen of Back Bay and the lace curtains of Roxbury is but a memory, perhaps not greatly missed. If the child's father is determined enough, however, there are a few steam-powered oddities to be seen—the little cog railway that runs up Mount Washington; two snorting

The steam locomotive was English-born, in the ideas of Newton, Newcomen, and Watt, but the first one actually to work was operated on a roadway in 1801 by Richard Trevithick, a Cornish mine operator. In 1804 he built the little engine below for a tramroad. It would haul twenty tons of iron. By the time Trevithick died penniless (as seems to be the case with many geniuses) in 1833, George Stephenson in England and Peter Cooper in America, among others, had proved that steam was here to stay.

ancients that climb about the workings of the Rock of Ages marble quarry in Barre, Vermont; a brace of narrow-gauge relics which operate at the Edaville Railroad Museum in South Carver, Massachusetts; an old vertical-piston type called a Shay that operates over a third of a mile at the Pine Creek Railroad near South Amboy, New Jersey. There is more of this kind of thing, but very little real steam railroading.

The first steam engine to go, interestingly enough, was the streamlined model, devised for the flashier passenger services. But the diesel, though first introduced only in 1925, has taken over nearly all the freight services too, so that to see real steam in action one must generally go to far places, to the mountains and the mining areas—in the Rockies on the Union

Pacific, where some of the "Big Boy" articulated engines still help ease long freights over the grades; in Canada; here and there in the Appalachians. An occasional coal-carrying road like the Norfolk & Western still diplomatically uses the customers' fuel. Some huge companies like the Pennsylvania have not quite finished the transition from steam; a few others, like the Nickel Plate, have steam locomotives too new to scrap. But it is very dangerous to use the present indicative these days in writing about such matters, for in the interval between setting down the words "there are . . ." and printing them, fatal changes are apt to take place.

At the peak in 1924, some 65,000 steam locomotives, aided by a few electric engines, carried on most of the

59

transportation business of America. Most of these steam engines were still on hand twenty years later, but now, all at once, there are scarcely two or three thousand. On the big Class I railroads—those with annual operating revenues over $3,000,000—nearly all the steam will go when the management can get delivery of diesels or, in some more embarrassing cases, raise the money for them. An economic law is at work which has no regard for romance: the diesel is cheaper to operate. And, apparently in a desire to underscore the point, every nerve and sinew has been bent toward making the diesel as ugly as possible.

Most of the surviving steamers, in a few years, will be the country cousins—motive power of branches, short lines, logging and quarry roads. ("Thank God for sand and gravel pits!" cried a railroad fancier's magazine the other day.) These survivors are generally little fellows of quaint and ancient cut, better adapted than the giants to short trains, light rails, fragile trestles, and uneven roadbeds. Often they are graying at the temples, to say the least. With a little renewing here and there and some deft cannibalizing of sister locomotives, however, a steam engine practically never wears out. *Smoky Mary*, brought over from England to a Louisiana line in 1832, operated satisfactorily for 100 years, and *John Bull*, built in 1831 by Robert Stephenson & Company at Newcastle-upon-Tyne, is still in working condition, although admittedly it spends most of its time these days just resting in the Smithsonian. In its own museum, the Baltimore & Ohio keeps a number of pre-Civil War engines like the *William Mason* ready to be steamed up and run out on the line whenever the movie-makers call.

The South, and particularly Georgia, has been a holdout in the era of the diesel, a kind of home to aging steam locomotives, but even here the new prosperity is falling on steam like a blight. And to find a *wood-burning* common carrier, one must travel a bit

west, to the Mississippi & Alabama Railroad, whose 27-mile line connects with the Gulf, Mobile & Ohio at Vinegar Bend, Alabama. On a corkscrew-track the M&A operates a fine old 2-6-2, or "Prairie" engine.

Locomotives, it should be explained, are classified for most purposes by their wheel arrangement. Thus the so-called "American" type of locomotive, of which many specimens are illustrated in these pages, is called a 4-4-0—signifying that there are four wheels under the front truck, four driving wheels, and no trailing wheels under the cab. Wheels under the tender, of course, are ignored. It tends to be the famous older (and smaller) types that survive—Consolidations (2-8-0); freight-hauling Moguls (2-6-0); ten-wheelers (4-6-0); Mikados (2-8-2); and Pacifics (4-6-2). Big as they are in relation to the little engines of the Civil War era, they are dwarfed by the great articulated Mallets, with their two sets of driving wheels, each rigged to its own set of cylinders, running in series as complex as 2-10-10-2.

The disappearance of a steam engine is rarely a publicized or even public event; it is a thing done privately in an undistinguished setting. One night old 567 rolls a way freight into the yard, uncouples, backs off on a rusty spur, and has her fires raked out and boilers drained for the last time. There she rusts a few weeks or months, depending on the market for scrap iron. Generally someone in authority comes by to chalk her boiler with a notice of disposition (or perhaps some more personal message like the "Goodbye, old Pal," one traveler observed in a Philadelphia yard) and eventually she goes to the torch. The public is on the highways and there is no audience to see the corpse borne off, like Hamlet's by the soldiers, with a dead march, drums, and peals of ordnance. But the drama is there, for this is the end of something entirely heroic, of a century and a quarter in which one great

THE PEALE MUSEUM, BALTIMORE

The first cars were basically coach bodies. The Winchester *(about 1832) was three Imlay coaches run together, built by Ross Winans, a horse trader who became a great engine and car builder. He patented the pivoted four-wheel trucks.*

Peter Cooper's Tom Thumb, *first American-built locomo on a regular railroad, ran its famous race with a horse*

60

invention transformed a scattering of towns and settlements into a united nation.

The story of America and the steam locomotive can be told in many ways. There is, for example, a tale of inventors frustrated and prophets ignored. Consider a strange genius named Oliver Evans, who was chattering about steam carriages as early as 1786. He built a strange, crawling, amphibious monster which he called the *Orukter Amphibole;* it moved on land to the Schuylkill River, waddled in and kept right on going. Naturally no one listened to a man like this when he suggested a wooden railway, with steam-drawn carriages to move between New York and Philadelphia at fifteen miles an hour. After him there was John Stevens of Hoboken, who operated the world's first steam ferry and, at the age of 76, designed and built with his own hands a toy engine which he operated on a circular track in his yard. This was 1825, the same year Stephenson's *Locomotion* appeared in England. But as early as 1812 Stevens had been telling all who would listen, a rather select company, that it would be better to build a railway than a canal between Albany and Lake Erie. If he had built the toy first, he might have been more convincing, but, at any rate, after 1825 the dam seemed to burst. Railroad projects sprang up everywhere, and railroading now became a story of inventors not only listened to but acclaimed. And the world had a new toy, viewed with horror by some and astonishment by others. Listen to an elegant gentleman of New York, George Templeton Strong, writing in 1839:

It's a great sight to see a large train get under way . . . As to the engine, the most pithy and expressive epithet I ever heard applied to it is "Hell-in-Harness." Just imagine such a concern rushing unexpectedly by a stranger to the invention on a dark night, whizzing and rattling and panting, with its fiery furnace gleaming in front, its chimney vomiting fiery smoke above, and its long train of cars rushing along behind like the body and tail of a gigantic dragon--or like the d——l himself—and all darting forward at the rate of twenty miles an hour. Whew!

When the rails came to Amherst, Emily Dickinson characteristically crouched in the woods to see the train move off and then rushed home to dash off a poem (*I like to hear it lap the miles, and lick the valleys up . . .*) Over in another wood lot, in Concord, Henry David Thoreau was opposed in principle but could not conceal a certain admiration:

. . . when I hear the iron horse make the hills echo with his snort like thunder, shaking the earth with his feet, and breathing fire and smoke from his nostrils . . . it seems as if the earth had got a race now worthy to inhabit it. If all were as it seems, and men made the elements their servants for noble ends!

There is a story of great feats of engineering too—of speed and danger, of wilderness tamed, rivers bridged, tunnels drilled, mountains surmounted. Here, for example, is Henry Flagler, 82 years old, achieving his dream at last, making the first ride across the railroad he built out to sea to reach Key West—twenty miles on embankments, seventeen on bridges. Here between Batavia and Buffalo is the famous speed trial of old 999, making 112.5 miles an hour, back in 1893. Out at Promontory, Utah, is the greatest denouement of all, as the Golden Spike goes down in 1869, in a burst of booze and oratory. Bret Harte writes a poem:

> *What was it the Engines said,*
> *Pilots touching, head to head*
> *Facing on a single track,*
> *Half a world behind each back?*

(They might have said: Achievements pass. For the rails bypass Promontory on a shorter route today, Mr. Flagler's railroad has been blown away, and old 999 has become a state fair exhibit. Where she passed, the

TEXT CONTINUED ON PAGE 126

History of the First Locomotives in America, BY W. H. BROWN, 1871

B&O in 1830, losing only when a belt slipped steam pressure sank. It was the horse's last victory.

Winans' later design, the Washington, *had a center aisle instead of the coach compartments; this set the custom for America although the British, respecting privacy, retained the older arrangement. This car joined the B&O in 1835.*

61

TWENTYFIVE TON PASSENGER ENGINE.
LAWRENCE MACHINE SHOP
LAWRENCE MASS.

Great builders and gaudy eight-wheelers

ENGINES OF THIS PLAN WEIGHING FROM 37000 TO 64000 LBS.
M. W. BALDWIN & CO, LOCOMOTIVE BUILDERS,
PHILADELPHIA.

Peter Cooper's experimental four-wheeled engine weighed barely a ton, used old musket barrels as boiler tubes, and applied power to only one axle. More power was needed and a number of great locomotive builders before long responded with the engine type that was pre-eminent throughout the nineteenth century, the sturdy "American" eight-wheeler. The forward truck was pivoted to help hold the sharp, bumpy curves; connecting rods added tractive power by turning all four main wheels into drivers. Bells, whistles, tight and efficient cylinders, covered cabs, oil head lamps, and other devices appeared; proud owners saw no need for somber colors. The Lawrence (upper left) was constructed in 1853, the gaudy Wyoming (above) shopped out by Richard Norris & Son of Philadelphia in 1857. The eight-wheeler below, the Highland Light, built in 1867 for the Cape Cod Central Railroad, typifies the work of the greatest artist in engine design, William Mason of Taunton, Massachusetts, who once observed that locomotives should "look somewhat better than cookstoves on wheels." The Tiger, all scroll and panel work (below left), was turned out in 1856 by Matthias Baldwin of Philadelphia, a jeweler who got into vastly successful locomotive building after making a miniature locomotive which operated on a small track in the Philadelphia museum of his friend Franklin Peale. One of Baldwin's durable engines, the Pioneer, built in 1836, with a few repairs was able to give reliable service under its own power during the Chicago Railroad Fair in 1949.

The 9:45 a.m. Accommodation, Stratford, Connecticut, *painted by E. L. Henry in 186* *recalls the day when the depot was the center of town, the engineer a great man, an*

ilroad Avenue a select address. Even the solitary Thoreau thought the depot atmos-
ere "electrifying" and called steam-car movements "the epochs in the village day."

The Lackawanna Valley *foreshadows as early as 1854 the new industrial look of America, and with it introduces an early specimen of the train watcher, or fan. The canvas was commissioned by George D. Phelps, first president of the Delaware, Lackawanna & Western Railroad, a penny-pinching patron of the arts who wished to immortalize his new round-house in Scranton, offering $75 for the job to a struggling young painter named George Inness. Mrs. Inness pressed her reluctant husband to accept and he, not trusting the steam cars, went to Scranton by stage coach, to be greeted by a demanding employer. For example, Phelps desired all the line's three engines in the picture, each lettered with the company's interminable name. For $75, said Inness, he could have only one, uninscribed. A single track then led into the roundhouse, but the president persuaded Inness to include others on the grounds that the line planned eventually to build them. Later the painting disappeared for many years, until Inness himself found it in Mexico City in 1892; he bought it back for a few dollars.*

Steam reshapes the landscape

SMITHSONIAN INSTITUTION

Held Up, *by N. H. Trotter, well expresses the confrontation between the locomotive and the Wild West it came to civilize. The buffalo herds, once estimated to number some fifteen millions, vanished after the continent-binding spike was driven in 1869, yet the tracks followed their paths. The bison always took the easiest grades.*

The marriage of the railroads and the cities brought its problems, not the least of which were murderous grade-crossings. Politicians, reformers, even novelists like Winston Churchill fought them bitterly. Here on a temporary trestle, in 1875, the New York Central crosses the Harlem wastes, bound for Grand Central Terminal.

In 1836 a combined highway and railroad bridge brought the Baltimore & Ohio into Harpers Ferry, crossing the Potomac and the Chesapeake & Ohio Canal (foreground). When this picture was made, in 1857, the B&O, via connecting lines, had just reached the Mississippi at St. Louis, Missouri. Beyond the river lay fresh perils, as shown in the highly imaginative 1870 scene below on the Little Rock & Fort Smith Railroad. The handsome engine McKay might scatter the red men, but it would never make that curve.

Though since overshadowed by the Moffat, Cascade, and other tunnels, the 4.73-mile Hoosac Tunnel in Massachusetts, on the line of the Fitchburg Railroad, was the wonder of the age when, after 21 years and 105 deaths, it was completed in 1876. This is one of its early advertising posters, when it served several railroads. Cutting through this east-west barrier in the Berkshires, the contractors, first to employ compressed air and nitroglycerine, encountered everything, even soluble rock which, when exposed to air, ran like quicksand. As one laborer said, it was "like trying to shovel live eels."

In the days of the Comstock Lode, the Afternoon Express on the Virginia & Truckee, the legendary mining railroad of Nevada, brought the gaudy new gentry of San Francisco up steep grades to the fleshpots of Virginia City. This painting by Howard Fogg depicts the late 1870's, and a string of Pullmans double-headed behind No. 12, the Genoa, and No. 11, the Reno. Genoa, built by Baldwin in 1872 and retired but not scrapped in 1912, is a fine example of the eight-wheeler in its prime. The V&T ran ancient engines and brightly painted wooden cars right down to the bitter end in 1950. Then the rolling stock went to Hollywood, but the rails, alas, joined the sorrowful roster of picturesque but vanished American short lines.

Double-headed behind little balloon-stacked engines, the Denver & Rio Grande Western three-foot gauge threads its precipitous way through the canyon of the Lost Souls from Durango to Silverton, Colorado. The date is 1885, but much the same sort of train still operates this route today, its ten period cars packed with enthusiasts well aware that they are riding the sole surviving narrow-gauge passenger route in America. Yet once upon a time, America boasted some 750 such lines.

70

Competition was real and advertising vigorous. Commodore Vanderbilt's New York Central gloried in its four new tracks.

The rival Erie had a six-foot gauge, Currier & Ives posters, and three rascals (Drew, Gould, and Fisk) running it. Before the great systems gobbled up the smaller ones, outlying routes like the Lake Shore (left) were independent. In 1856, when this poster came out, the Erie had just reached the lake whose name it bears. Its broad-gauge cars could go no farther. These were times when railroad managements vaunted their steam engines and actually cared, as someone has remarked, about the passenger element.

71

Back in 1909, when this highly symbolic chromolithograph was printed for the adornment of depot and schoolroom walls, steam ruled the world of transportation, undaunted by flimsy aircraft or newfangled automobiles. Earth satellites were provided strictly by the Almighty.

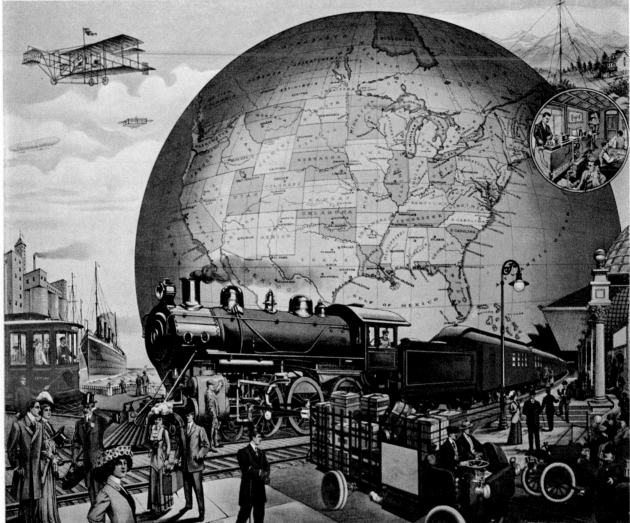

FOR ASSISTANCE WITH THE
PREPARATION OF THIS ARTICLE
WE EXPRESS OUR THANKS TO
EDGAR T. MEAD

Where it can be found at all, the steam locomotive today is generally a genteel relic operating on some weed-grown branch like the Bellefonte Central at right, an eighteen-mile Pennsylvania short line. "No regular passenger service operated," reads the small, bleak notice of the company in the Official Railway Guide, *but this does not deceive close students of that publication. All it means is that passengers are urged to stay away but will be carried if they insist. So, the railroads hope, they will eventually totally discourage a business they can no longer afford to maintain. But while they last, operations of this kind somehow evoke an earlier age of railroading and a gentler, slower-moving past.*

A re-examination

by GERALD W. JOHNSON

Every time there's a thunderstorm around Marshfield, they say you can hear his rolling voice in the hollows of the sky. And they say that if you go to his grave and speak loud and clear, "Dan'l Webster—Dan'l Webster!" the ground'll begin to shiver and the trees begin to shake. And after a while you'll hear a deep voice saying, "Neighbor, how stands the Union?" Then you better answer the Union stands as she should, rock bottomed and copper sheathed, one and indivisible, or he's liable to rear right out of the ground. At least, that's what I was told when I was a youngster.

You see, for a while, he was the biggest man in the country. He never got to be President, but he was the biggest man. There were thousands that trusted in him right next to God Almighty, and they told stories about him and all the things that belonged to him that were like the stories of patriarchs and such. They said, when he stood up to speak, stars and stripes came right out in the sky, and once he spoke against a river and made it sink into the ground. A man with a mouth like a mastiff, a brow like a mountain and eyes like burning anthracite—that was Dan'l Webster in his prime.

The Devil and Daniel Webster
by Stephen Vincent Benét

GREAT MAN ELOQUENT

To an emotional people, it is not the senator, not the corporation lawyer,

not the secretary of state, but the poet's Daniel Webster who still lives

For more than a hundred years everybody has been writing about Daniel Webster and some have written well, but it can be plausibly argued that only one has written truthfully. There are twelve formal lives of Webster listed in the *Dictionary of American Biography,* and this takes no account of shorter studies by historians, philosophers, journalists, orators, and every known brand of politician. Few Americans have been more assiduously studied over so long a period.

But if effective history is such knowledge of the past as modifies contemporary thought and action, then one must agree with William A. Dunning that truth in history is not necessarily what happened, but what men believe happened, for it is on their beliefs that they act. What the vast majority of Americans believe about Daniel Webster is only slightly related to the mass of documentary evidence that scholarship has turned up; but it is not on that account to be dismissed as untrue. Fact and truth are related, but they are not identical, which accounts for our ability to weld "sophist" and "moron" into one word—the eternal sophomore who may acquire massive factual knowledge, but whom truth eludes.

The pedestrian writers who have dealt with Webster, even Gamaliel Bradford the Younger, even Samuel Hopkins Adams, have been hamstrung by their reliance on demonstrable fact as the key to essential truth. Not until the man had been almost a century dead did one who was no pedestrian, but a rider on Pegasus, have the boldness to repudiate fact altogether

and present Webster not as he was prior to 1852, but as he is now.

There was indeed a senator named Webster who represented Massachusetts, but he is dead. There was a fabulously successful corporation lawyer, but he too is dead, and who cares? There was a man, curiously compounded of wisdom and folly, who suffered adulation for his folly and denunciation for his wisdom, who tried to understand this world and failed, as we all do, and who, as we all must, eventually died.

There never was, in visible, tangible flesh, a man who performed the feats attributed to the hero of Stephen Vincent Benét's allegory, *The Devil and Daniel Webster.* The story asserts that this advocate, as counsel for the defense in the case of *Satan v. Jabez Stone,* won a verdict and, incidentally, his own salvation from a jury composed of the twelve greatest villains in American history, because the advocate's fiery patriotism burned away his client's and his own offenses. Nevertheless, in the eyes of posterity this fictional pleader has been the living Webster rather than the subject of the twelve biographies.

For the poet Benét did not create this figure any more than the poet Homer created the figure of Achilles. Like Homer,

> 'E'd 'eard men sing by land and sea;
> An' what 'e thought 'e might require,
> 'E went an' took—

to distill it in the alembic of poetic art and produce the Immortal. He gathered up the pre-existing legends and traditions, stripped off their crudity and added grace and dignity to a figure that the folk imagination had limned before Benét was born. But in so doing he revealed the potency of Daniel Webster in the modern world more precisely than any factual historian has revealed it.

The potency does not rest upon the statutes Webster drew, the contracts he negotiated, nor the politics he played. It is based upon his success as the establisher of moods, and that kind of success is never attested by documents. On the contrary, the documentary evidence frequently seems to contradict it, which is so much the worse for the documentary evidence. It is just this failure of the letter to capture the spirit that is the ruin of biographers and historians and the opportunity of poets. Talking of Daniel Webster conveys little that is of importance today; it was when Benét began to sing that the still surviving power and glory appeared.

The industrious pedestrians have uncovered the facts down to astonishingly small details. A New Hampshire farmer, wise beyond most of his generation, spared one of his many children the hard labor of the fields because the boy was physically sickly, although mentally precocious. Instead, the boy was sent to the best teachers available and eventually to Dartmouth College. He justified this indulgence twice, first by helping one of his brothers through college, and later by abandoning a promising professional career to care for his parents in their declining years. But the lofty intelligence, like the Scriptural city set upon a hill, could not be hid; at 31 the man was in the House of Representatives from New Hampshire. This was in 1813, just before the final wreck of the Federalist party in the Hartford Convention at the beginning of 1815. With his party shot from under him, the young man repaired to Boston in 1816 and in ten years had pushed his income from legal practice to $15,000 a year—in purchasing power the equivalent of $50,000 to $75,000 today. He went to the Senate in 1827, became secretary of state in 1841, returned to the Senate in 1845, became secretary of state again in 1850, and died in 1852.

Like every first-rate American who goes into politics, he wished to be President of the United States, and like most first-rate men he suffered the mortification of seeing second-raters chosen in his stead. During his time in Washington, Webster saw ten individuals occupying the White House and knew in his heart that he was superior to eight of them. No doubt he thought he was superior to the other two, Madison and Jackson, but history disallows that claim.

The second most brilliant period of American politics was beginning when Webster entered Congress, and he was, in popular estimation, one third of it. That was, of course, the same kind of exaggeration that gives the most brilliant period one half to Jefferson and the other half to Hamilton, although they were merely the two brightest stars in a galaxy. In the second period, Webster, Clay, and Calhoun outshone all other members of Congress, but not by much. Benton, Hayne, John Quincy Adams, Van Buren, Marcy, and John Randolph were no dim lights, and outside of Congress stood the gigantic figures of Andrew Jackson and John Marshall.

Of the illustrious trio, Webster was the latest arrival and, on technicalities, the least successful. All of them made Cabinet rank, but Calhoun was Vice President for seven years and Clay was three times a candidate for President, twice as the nominee of a major party. Thus it may fairly be said that both came closer to the White House than Webster did, although none reached it.

Without doubt Webster was refused even a nomination because his affiliations made him politically unavailable. He was the recognized spokesman of Big Business, and even at that early date party leaders were sure that nomination of such a candidate would be party suicide. It was not regarded as scandalous for a member of Congress to continue to serve his rich clients even—indeed especially—before government agencies, but it was regarded as a political handicap, and Webster's party was never strong enough to assume that handicap. Curiously enough, this favorite advocate of astute businessmen had so little "money sense" that in spite of an income that was, for the time, a huge one, he was perpetually in debt and therefore never able to break away from subservience to wealth.

But there is another aspect of this man that is even more curious. The spokesman of Big Business, the great corporation lawyer, is a familiar figure. There is always at least one in Congress, frequently half a dozen in the Administration, and they are conspicuous, often dominant, figures, so we know the type or think we do; and the common opinion is that the agent of Big Business, whatever his merits, is decidedly a cold fish, emphatically not the kind of material out of which popular heroes are made. Is it imaginable that a poet could have woven a folk tale around Thomas C. Platt or Nelson W. Aldrich or Elihu Root or Andrew Mellon? But Webster was legendary even before his death, and since that event the legend has grown until it overshadows that of Henry Clay, much the more popular figure while he lived.

The inescapable inference is that there was a link between the ordinary American and this extraordinary individual, some quality that enables the common man to feel a kinship with Webster that he never feels with any cold fish. The easy assumption is that his faults endeared him to the sinful majority, and no doubt they did to some extent.

> Dan Webster stoked his boilers with brown jugs of apple cider,
> And when he made a speech he yanked the spigot open wider.
> Sing ho! those spirited debates, bereft of all restrictions,
> When statesmen carried on their hip the strength of their convictions,

is evidence that his fondness for the bottle passed into the legend, and his amorous adventures, probably apocryphal, have been the theme of innumerable smoking-room stories. But these things the people regard with indulgence, not with approval; and somewhere in the American mind there is a deep and powerful approval of Daniel Webster, and a proprietary pride.

Yet when one examines any of his specific activities it seems far away and long ago, frequently without much logical significance even at the time. The celebrated Reply to Hayne, for example, was not a reply to Hayne at all. It was the evocation of a mood, not the refutation of an argument, a histrionic, not a logical triumph. "Liberty *and* Union, now and forever, one and inseparable!" had nothing whatever to do with the points that Hayne had raised, but it stirred up a tremendous emotional reaction against the idea of disunion. Logic frequently eludes the grasp of the masses, but they understand feeling instantly; and they understood Webster. His heart was in the right place.

At least four of his exploits have affected and still affect the destinies of every man and woman in the United States, and each of them was of the same order—the establishment of a mood rather than the defense of a thesis. These were the Dartmouth College case, the case of *McCulloch v. Maryland,* the negotiation of the Webster-Ashburton Treaty, and the Compromise of 1850.

Examined in the cold light of reason all of these

are without significance as of the year 1957; but in the warm glow of emotion it is apparent that each of them grips us today with an unbreakable hold. None was the work of Daniel Webster alone, but he was an operative force in all four, and he remains an operative force to this day.

The Dartmouth College case established the sanctity of contract. The case revolved around an effort by the state of New Hampshire to move in and take control of a college that it had chartered, perpetually, as a private institution; which, Webster argued, was an effort by the state to repudiate its own contract, which not even a sovereign has a right to do. The court presumably was moved by the logic of the argument, but Webster's passing remark, "She is small, but there are those who love her," hit the country with an impact that no kind of logical exposition could achieve. The fact that this case came dangerously close to repealing the Statutes of Mortmain and delivering the future into economic bondage was something for jurisconsults to worry over; the people saw in it only the rescue of cherished and threatened institutions, and that mood has persisted through all the discomforts that immortality of corporations has brought upon us.

The case of *McCulloch v. Maryland* successfully asserted the right of judicial review of legislation. Logically, it is untenable, but practically it has worked, and that is enough for the common man. Possibly the hard core of that decision was John Marshall's determination to bow his arrogant head to no man, even at the behest of the Aristotelian syllogism. That is as it may be. But deep in the heart of the common man is a conviction that logic is an invention of schoolmasters that bears precious little relation to life as he lives it; so if the advocate in this case departed from the accepted rules he did not thereby offend the typical American. Rather, he aroused a fraternal understanding among men more intent upon devising a workable method than upon making their reasoning conform to BARBARA or FRESISON. So even in this legalistic matter they have felt close to Daniel Webster; and the mood then established, the feeling that the Constitution must be made to work, even if it has to be bent into the shape of a pretzel, has persisted from that day to this.

The Webster-Ashburton Treaty is one of the most remarkable in the history of diplomacy, not for what is contained so much as for the manner in which it was nego-

77

tiated. Alexander Baring, Lord Ashburton, was sent over in 1842 as a special envoy to take up with Webster, then secretary of state, a number of issues in dispute between the United States and Great Britain, the most important of which was the boundary line between Maine and Canada. That line had never been properly surveyed, but simply marked out on maps supposed to be attached to the treaty, but which had somehow become detached. The matter then hinged on discovery of the right map and both parties ransacked the archives.

Through the agency of Jared Sparks, in Paris, Webster was supplied with a map said to have been marked by Benjamin Franklin and given to the French ministry—and it knocked the bottom out of the American claim. About the same time someone discovered in the British archives a map supposed to have been marked for the information of King George III—and it knocked the bottom out of the British claim. But neither negotiator suspected the existence of the other map; all either knew was that his own position was exceedingly precarious.

Thus each went into the discussions warily and with the most scrupulous regard for punctilio. When the citizens of Maine threatened to become obstreperous, Webster privately showed their leaders the Jared Sparks map, and they instantly subsided. So, since neither principal could risk being adamant, the dickering and dealing proceeded smoothly to a conclusion reasonably satisfactory to both sides.

But much more was accomplished than the boundary settlement, much that does not appear in the written records and, indeed, was never formally admitted by either side. This accomplishment was a marked softening of our diplomatic contacts with Great Britain. His lordship discovered that the American, far from being a raucous and semiliterate backwoodsman, was an urbane and gentlemanly fellow. The American, on his part, discovered that a noble lord is not necessarily arrogant and supercilious, but may be

The Reply to Hayne

This is the scene where the famous phrase about Liberty and Union was uttered: Webster, in the classic stance, replies to Senator Robert Y. Hayne of South Carolina, who is sitting at left center, just to the right of the ancient lawgiver in curls. Vice President Calhoun presides. Mrs. Webster is one of the watching ladies, and the artist, G. P. A. Healy, has put in other celebrities elsewhere in the gallery seats. The date is January 26, 1830; the issue, the interminable issue—states' rights. Hear the great organ peal:
". . . When my eyes shall be turned to behold for the last time the sun in heaven, may I not see him shining on the broken and dishonored fragments of a once glorious Union; on states dissevered, discordant, belligerent; on a land rent with civil feuds, or drenched, it may be, in fraternal blood! Let their last feeble and lingering glance rather behold the gorgeous ensign of the Republic, now known and honored throughout the earth, still full high advanced, its arms and trophies streaming in their original lustre, not a stripe erased or polluted, not a single star obscured, bearing for its motto no such miserable interrogatory as 'What is all this worth?' nor those other words of delusion and folly, 'Liberty first and Union afterwards'; but everywhere, spread all over in characters of living light, blazing on all its ample folds, as they float over the sea and over the land, and in every wind under the whole heavens, that other sentiment, dear to every true American heart —Liberty and Union, now and forever, one and inseparable!"

a reasonable, fair-minded character with whom it is a pleasure to do business. The discovery that each was carefully polite because he distrusted his own case came long afterward and did not destroy the mood created in 1842.

Of course this mood was reinforced by many other factors, but without doubt it was helped along by the Webster-Ashburton negotiations; and 115 years later it still persists. Before that date our contacts with the British were, as a rule, unpleasantly rough, but since then they have been the smoothest of all. Even the Anglophobes among us feel the effect and hold that while to swindle the English may be permissible and even praiseworthy, it must always be done with a certain suavity amid expressions of the utmost good will. Daniel Webster had much to do with establishing that mood and therein he touches your life and mine.

But it was on March 7, 1850, that Daniel Webster probably saved the Union and ruined himself by rising to greatness. The aftermath of the Mexican War had had the usual effect of war's aftermath—it had driven the more emotional elements of the population into raving insanity. It is at such times that formerly gentle souls turn into vipers, and formerly shrewd fellows take to a braying that drowns the voice of reason. As far as the United States is concerned certainly, and perhaps as regards other nations as well, the loss of blood and treasure that attends the actual conflict has never been as permanently injurious to the nation as the loss of common sense and common decency that follows the cessation of hostilities.

The Mexican affair had ended in 1848, and by 1850 mass hysteria had reached its height. In Congress John C. Calhoun, for the South, and William H. Seward, for the North, were no longer arguing, they were merely screeching; and each was attended by a rabble of noise-makers whose din all but obliterated calm counsel. It was plain, all too appallingly plain, that any small spark might set off an explosion that would destroy the Union.

CONTINUED ON PAGE 121

The undimmed appeal of

THE GIBSON GIRL

By AGNES ROGERS

In the dear, nostalgic days of the 1890's and early 1900's a vibrant, radiant young woman took the country by storm. She was the Gibson Girl, a brilliant invention, something quite new. She was lovely, animated, and unquestionably American. And today, though four change-filled decades have passed, more men are still in love with her than you might think.

Why is her appeal still so potent? She was far removed from our current notions of the ideal American woman. She was not particularly bright and not highly educated. She was not politically informed, and her social conscience, in present-day terms, was dormant. She could not cook or manage a home, nor did she resemble today's pin-up girl, whose charms are so candidly revealed in certain large-circulation magazines.

Yet even now she evokes worshipful sighs from men too young ever to have known anyone resembling her. One reason, I think, is that the Gibson Girl was forever a girl—forever young and beautiful. She was femininity incarnate without being (in today's terms) sexy. And nowadays, when sex is portrayed in such blatant detail, it is refreshing to be given the promise of future raptures rather than the play-by-play accounts of bedroom romps in current novels.

In any discussion of the Gibson Girl there is a word, now taboo, that one cannot avoid. She was a lady. In fact, John Ames Mitchell, founder of *Life* (the original one), explained that one of the reasons he accepted the first drawings of Charles Dana Gibson was that he could draw a lady. The Gibson Girl represents the rosiest aspect of Society (with a capital S) at a period in American life when Society was more clearly defined, less complex, and far more admired than it is today. Gibson himself, by virtue of his birth, his engaging personality, and his agreeable manners, had the entree to New York's

TEXT CONTINUED ON PAGE 97

Her infinite variety

FORE!

THE AMERICAN GIRL TO ALL THE WORLD

THE AMERICAN GIRL ABROAD

HERE SHE IS, CHAPERONED BY A REAL DUCHESS, WITH TWO NOBLEMEN OF AN-
CIENT LINEAGE READY TO MARRY HER, AND YET HER HAPPINESS IS NOT COMPLETE.

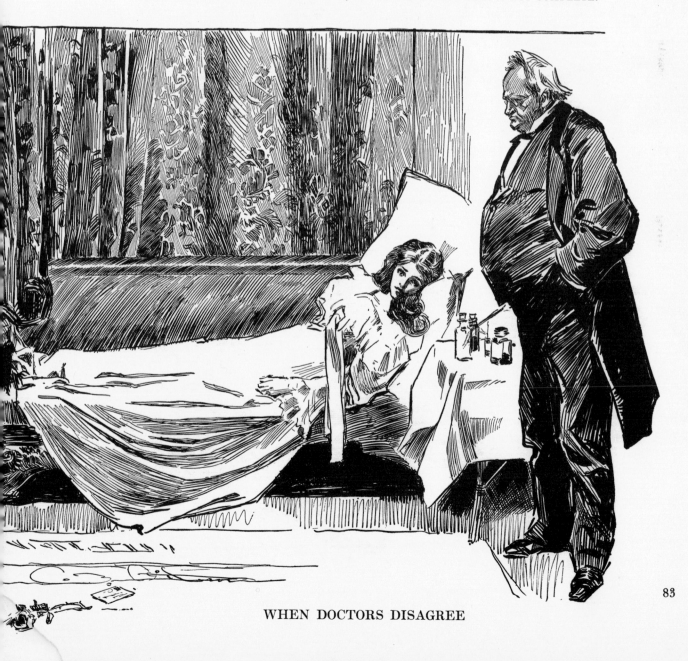

WHEN DOCTORS DISAGREE

Man proposes, She disposes

MELTING

PICTURESQUE AMERICA
ANYWHERE ALONG THE COAST

THE WEAKER SEX

THE YOUNG MAN IMAGINES HIMSELF THE LATEST VICTIM OF SOME FAIR ENTOMOLOGIST.

LIFE'S VAUDEVILLE

"I'LL BE A SISTER TO YOU."

HEARTS ARE TRUMPS

HE HAS DIFFICULTY KEEPING HIS MIND ON THE GAME AND REPEATEDLY TRUMPS HIS PARTNER'S TRICKS.

Everything brings them together...

ALL BROKEN UP

ANOTHER COLLISION WITH SERIOUS RESULTS

TWO'S COMPANY,
THREE'S A CROWD

THE OTHER MAN SHOULD
REMEMBER THAT HE IS A CROWD.

A LITTLE INCIDENT

SHOWING THAT EVEN INANIMATE OBJECTS CAN ENTER INTO THE SPIRIT OF THE GAME.

...Or almost together

THE PARTY WALL

A CASTLE IN THE AIR

THESE YOUNG GIRLS WHO MARRY OLD MILLIONAIRES SHOULD STOP DREAMING.

ANOTHER MONOPOLY

WIRELESS TELEGRAPHY

Love conquers all

THE LAST GUEST

TEXT CONTINUED FROM PAGE 80

highest social circles and found the best it had to offer highly sympathetic. By "best" I mean a group of congenial people of established family, inherited wealth, and cultivated tastes, who employed their leisure in genuinely graceful (not "gracious") living.

Gibson hated snobbishness; the only person he lampooned openly was Ward McAllister, who, it will be remembered, numbered the people worth knowing in New York as 400, that being the capacity of Mrs. Astor's ballroom. Gibson also hated the vulgarity of those newly rich who attempted to buy their way into elite circles. His picture entitled "Mrs. Steele Poole's Housewarming" is a not-very-subtle reference to the onslaught of newly made millionaires from Pittsburgh—where steel combines were proliferating—on New York Society.

The Society that Gibson approved of, and in which he was most at home, was the old guard—scornful of public entertainers and of the attentions of the press. A lady's name appeared in newspapers just three times: when she was born, when she married, and when she died. That Society stoutly resisted the idea that wealth and position are synonymous, confident that in itself it represented all that was best and most important in American life. And many people of less exalted position agreed.

It is hard today to realize how widespread was the interest in the doings of the socially prominent and how faithfully the magazines reported them. The American public read avidly and respectfully of the "at home" given by Mr. and Mrs. Cornelius Vanderbilt in Newport in 1902, where an illuminated midway had been set up with Negro dancers, a shooting gallery, singing girls, and other exhibits found in amusement parks, and at the far end, a theater where the New York cast and scenery of a current Broadway musical, *The Wild Rose,* had been transported for the evening. Or a dinner dance given by Mrs. Ogden Goelet, where in one cotillion figure 700 gardenias were distributed from a Russian sleigh.

The American public saw nothing to censure in the fact that several New York hostesses were able to serve a dinner for 100 guests on a few hours' notice—no informal buffet, but the customary seven- or eight-course affair with appropriate wines. Servants there were, to be sure, in task-force strength, some large country places being staffed by as many as fifty or sixty, including gardeners and grooms. These entertainments were not paid for from expense accounts. The cost came from the host's private purse.

It was against this glittering background that the Gibson Girl—beautiful, queenly, confident—moved in triumph.

Yet, though her habitat was high society, she was the darling of the less affluent as well. When I say that she took the country by storm, I am speaking nearly literally. In countless houses all over the land prints of Gibson drawings were hung on the walls and Gibson's long red picture books were on parlor tables. Manufacturers labeled "Gibson Girl" all manner of women's clothes—shirtwaists with the "Gibson pleat" running from shoulder to waist in a tapering line, skirts, hats, riding stocks, etc. Spoons, plates, even wall paper were ornamented with her face. Her serene likeness was burned—through the cunning craft of pyrography—into wood or leather table tops, glove boxes, umbrella stands, and any other household equipment with a surface large enough to accommodate it. Songs —"Why Do They Call Me A Gibson Girl?"—were written in her honor. *Tableaux Vivants,* a favorite entertainment at bazaars and other amateur performances, were based on a series of Gibson drawings, usually familiar to the entire audience.

And together with this nation-wide recognition of the Gibson Girl's charms came a tidal wave of emulation. Girls all over the country wanted to be as nearly like her as possible. They dressed like her; they wore their hair like her. "You can always tell," wrote Robert Bridges, "when a girl is taking the Gibson Cure by the way she fixes her hair. I've watched them go through the whole scale from Psyche knots to pompadours, to Bath Buns, to side waves with a bewitching part in the middle." Nor did the young men escape her influence. The Gibson man was usually clean-shaven (as were the artist himself and his father before him) and strong-jawed, the precursor of the Arrow Collar man. Many a luxuriant moustache was shaved off. The Gibson Girl was tall. Young men stood erect to gain inches.

Just who was the original model for the Gibson Girl? Many people have said that she was Mrs. Gibson, the lovely Irene Langhorne from Virginia, one of four sisters of legendary beauty. It is true that after their marriage—and a spectacularly happy marriage it proved to be—on November 7, 1895, Mrs. Gibson often posed for her husband, but the Gibson Girl was already in existence before then. She was a composite, not an individual. The artist's earliest models were often young society girls whom he knew and who were only too happy to come, carefully chaperoned, naturally, to the attractive young man's studio for a sitting. (The original Gibson Man, by the way, was Richard Harding Davis, Gibson's friend and author of numerous stories illustrated by the artist.)

Everybody agrees that the Gibson Girl connotes romance. Love, courtship, and marriage are the themes that engaged Gibson's liveliest interest. And he was truly romantic about his darling creation. It revolted him to think of a girl's being married off for money, especially to an old man, and this subject appears time after time. His fury was roused also by those international alliances in which American dollars were exchanged for a foreign title. The vogue started in the seventies, when lovely Jennie Jerome, daughter of a New York banker, married Lord Randolph Churchill (and, happily for the world, later produced the mighty Winston Churchill). It had become almost an epidemic in the nineties and gave rise to the term "Dollar Princesses." In its November, 1903, issue, *McCall's* published a list of fifty-seven marriages between American women and foreign noblemen. The list included such resplendent unions as that of Lord Curzon and Miss Daisy Leiter, Count Boni de Castellane and Miss Anna Gould, the Marquis de Tallyrand-Périgord and Miss Curtis, the Duc de la Rochefoucauld and Miss Mattie Mitchell, the Earl of Oxford and Miss Louise Corbin, and the Duke of Roxburghe and Miss May Goelet.

Of course there must have been some love matches among the fifty-seven, but it was apparently significant to Gibson that a contract signed November 6, 1895, when Consuelo Vanderbilt married the Duke of Marlborough, contained the following passage:

"Whereas, a marriage is intended between the said Duke of Marlborough and the said Consuelo Vanderbilt . . . the sum of two million five hundred thousand dollars in fifty thousand shares of the Beech Creek Railway Company, on which an annual payment of four per cent is guaranteed by the New York Central Railroad Company, is transferred this day to the trustees. And shall, during the joint lives of the said Duke of Marlborough, Consuelo Vanderbilt, pay the income of the said sum of two million five hundred thousand dollars, unto the Duke of Marlborough for his life, and after the death of the said Duke of Marlborough, shall pay the income of the said trust fund unto the said Consuelo for life. . . ."

For the most part, Gibson portrays the foreigners who fall prostrate at the feet of the Great American Girl as rather seedy specimens, but very occasionally he permits himself to show us a presentable Englishman. This may have been a gesture toward his wife's sister, Nancy Langhorne, who married Lord Astor. Or the change may have resulted from his own trips to Britain, during which he fraternized with and was feted by the foe and learned that most English lords preferred to marry English ladies.

It is often said that the American girl prior to World War I lived a pretty dull life, at least a carefully confined one, and mostly indoors. Not so the Gibson Girl. As early as the nineties we see her on the tennis court, on the golf links, on a bicycle, even driving a motor car. To be sure, when she went into the water at the seashore, she wore a decorous bathing suit (with the obligatory stockings). But she wore no bathing cap. Either she never got her head under water or Gibson couldn't bear to hide her crowning glory.

Actually, by the turn of the century, the outdoor life was an accepted thing in upper class circles, chiefly along the eastern seaboard. With the exception of bicycling (that great liberator of American women as a whole) most outdoor sports suitable for mixed company began as diversions for the well-to-do and gradually filtered downward in the social scale to become the property of the masses. Public tennis courts and golf courses were many years in the future. The automobile, in its early years, was a rich man's toy rather than the necessary adjunct of every American family which it is today.

So, when Gibson put a racket or a niblick in his heroine's graceful hand, he was reflecting the mores of that small sector of the social scene that most interested him. In his preoccupation with romance, he was also quick to see that these games offered ideal situations for unchaperoned but wholly respectable association between the sexes. An afternoon on the links— what an admirable setting for courtship! One of his best-known drawings, entitled "Is A Caddy Always Necessary?" depicts a young couple seated glumly on a bunker, hoping their gangling young club carrier will realize their desire to be alone. One may be assured that even if these goddesses could handily defeat their adoring opponents, they were far too tactful to do so.

Oddly enough, when the Gay Nineties are revived today in revue skit or greeting card, the spectacle bears no resemblance to the Gibson Girl or her circle. All the men have handle-bar moustaches and the girls are made up as Sweet Rosie O'Grady or Mamie O'Rourke. In other words, they are low life. Very merry, very gay, but definitely low life. The Gibson Girl was just as definitely high life. Moreover, whereas these jovial modern revivals from the Bowery are comic valentines, the Gibson Girl defies caricature. The short-haired, short-skirted hoyden of the twenties, the flapper immortalized by John Held, was something of a caricature to begin with. It is almost impossible to exaggerate her. For quite another reason, the Gibson Girl remains as she was created, immaculate and bewitching. To burlesque her would be sacrilege.

Agnes Rogers, associate editor of the Reader's Digest Condensed Book Club, is the author of Women Are Here to Stay, From Man to Machine, *and, with her late husband, Frederick Lewis Allen, of* The American Procession *and* I Remember Distinctly.

LODGE

CORTELYOU

WHITE

MC CORMICK

PINCHOT

BUTLER

JOHNSON

PERKINS

T. R.
ON THE TELEPHONE

By private wire from Oyster Bay Roosevelt angled for the 1916 Progressive and

Republican nominations, but his strategy backfired and killed the Progressive party

Edited by JOHN A. GARRATY

On June 7, 1916, the national conventions of the Progressive and Republican parties were about to open simultaneously in Chicago. Of the many presidential candidates who would be suggested at the Republican convention only two, ex-President Theodore Roosevelt and Supreme Court Justice Charles Evans Hughes, seemed to have a real chance of being nominated. Almost to a man, the Progressive delegates were determined to name Roosevelt, who had fashioned the party in righteous indignation four years earlier, when William Howard Taft had "stolen" the Republican nomination that Roosevelt believed his.

Defeat had thinned the Progressive ranks, but the survivors were zealous and loyal. Roosevelt, whatever his personal wishes, felt a sense of obligation to them. Ideally he would have liked to be nominated by both parties, which would have been a tacit admission by the Republicans that they had mistreated him in 1912. Failing that, he wanted to see some other candidate chosen whom both groups could endorse. President Wilson, fortified by his New Freedom domestic reforms and by his obviously sincere dedication to keeping the United States out of the bloody European war, would be a formidable opponent even for the combined Republican and Progressive forces; if they were split, he would be well-nigh invincible. Most sensible politicians in both the Progressive and Re-

publican parties were eager to unite.

Each side had one mighty asset the other lacked. The Republicans had a powerful political organization, but no candidate of national stature or appeal. The Progressives were woefully lacking in experienced workers at the precinct level, but they had in Roosevelt a proved and colorful national leader. While both parties were willing to work for union, neither was willing to surrender much of its independence, and on the eve of the conventions no real progress had been made. For this reason the confusion common to all national conventions was even greater than usual, for, with the fate of both parties at stake, the politicians worked frantically and often at cross-purposes. Understanding Roosevelt's key role and knowing that important decisions would have to be made on short notice, his chief representative at Chicago, the retired Morgan banker George W. Perkins, had installed a private telephone line between his own rooms at the Blackstone Hotel and Roosevelt's home in Oyster Bay, Long Island. To allay Roosevelt's fears that he would be misquoted, Perkins had his secretary, Miss Mary Kihm, monitor the conversations. Never before published, Miss Kihm's transcript, from which the following excerpts are taken, reveals the mounting tension of that hectic week and lights up the events that went on behind the scenes.

*   *   *

Monday and Tuesday, June 5 and 6
With the formal opening of the conventions two days away, Republican and Progressive leaders began to assemble in Chicago. As they canvassed the delegates, it became increasingly clear that the leading Republican candidate was Hughes. Roosevelt did not want to support him, partly because of his own ambitions and partly because he felt that Hughes was, if not actually pro-German, at least insufficiently enthusiastic for preparedness and "Americanism" in the face of the European war. Hughes had taken the position that as a judge he ought not to seek the nomination—a stand that, however sincerely held, enabled him to be discreetly silent on the issues of the day. Roosevelt, therefore, argued that he could not support Hughes until he knew where the Justice stood on these issues.

Perkins worked assiduously among the delegates before the conventions opened. Among conservative Republicans he found Senator Boies Penrose of Pennsylvania and Senator Henry Cabot Lodge of Massachusetts willing to support Roosevelt. Lodge and Roosevelt had been friends for more than 30 years; not so Penrose, but his bluff remark, "I don't want

Hughes; I cannot do business with Hughes; I can do business with Roosevelt," was very encouraging to Perkins.

At 12:30 A.M. on June 6, Perkins put Penrose and Lodge on the private wire to Oyster Bay.

Penrose: This Hughes proposition has assumed proportions none of us dreamed of before we came here. . . . I do not suppose more than a quarter of [the delegates] are here yet. Mr. Perkins is making a careful canvass and so am I, to see where we are at. . . . Have you any suggestions to make?

Roosevelt: No, Senator, except that I want to say one thing. Supposing that matters come about so that I am nominated; I want to say to you what I have said to Mr. Perkins . . . that you will be the leader in the Senate at that time.

Penrose: . . . That side of it is not the question with me. . . . I really do not think the question of patronage, while a factor with a percentage of the delegates, is the controlling factor at present. . . . There is a general desire to win. . . . Lodge is here. Think it would be a good thing for you to talk with him. . . .

Lodge: Hello, Theodore.

Roosevelt: Hello, Cabot Lodge.

Lodge: It is a very mixed up situation we have here. . . .

The thing lies just this way: It looks like the nomination of Hughes [by the Republicans]. There is no enthusiasm for him at all but there is a wide-spread feeling that he can be more easily elected than any one else. Now to nominate you in that convention—I do not know if the votes are there or not. Of course if the Progressives nominate you before we act, that blows our plans all up and destroys them; you know there is a lunatic fringe to the Progressive party—I use your own words.

Roosevelt: Rightly said.

Lodge: . . . It is going to be either you or Hughes, in my judgment. . . . It is very hard to get at the convention. You know these delegates are all elected independently and are uninstructed and they cannot be handed around and delivered. . . . The question is how many votes they can show for you, and that I do not know. . . .

Roosevelt: As far as my personal interests are concerned, if they do not nominate me I shall breathe a sigh of relief. I have no ambition to go into a purely political campaign. . . . I can earnestly say I am not interested in my personal welfare at all; but in international matters and in the present situation I know I am worth two of Hughes.

Late that evening John T. King, Republican national committeeman from Connecticut, made the same point to Roosevelt.

King: . . . I am very much afraid of this Hughes situation tonight.

Roosevelt: I think myself that is the way the thing is drifting.

King: Yes, very fast, and if [Hughes's opponents] do not get a program pretty quick it is going to be almost impossible to stop it. . . . Here is the stand I am taking, Colonel: No matter whether the two conventions can get together or not as far as politics is concerned it is the duty of us fellows to stop Hughes by all means. Even though the Progressives and the Republicans cannot get together there is no sense in nominating Hughes. So let us go down on that principle.

Between them, Lodge and King had outlined the course which Roosevelt's supporters were to follow for the rest of the week: to stop Hughes and to seek to build support among the Republicans for Roosevelt or for a candidate he could support; and simultaneously to hold off the eager Progressives from immediately nominating Roosevelt, behind whom the Republicans, in their convention, were not yet ready to unite.

Roosevelt spoke again with Lodge regarding a speech Hughes had given at a girls' school. Then he brought up the question of who should place his name in nomination at the Republican convention:

Lodge: How are you, all right?

Roosevelt: Right as a trivet. Very much amused by Hughes's speech. It is exactly like a Wilson speech to the Colonial Dames. . . . Now I wish to ask whether it would not be a good thing to have [Senator Albert] Fall of New Mexico * nominate me?

Lodge: He would do it very well.

Roosevelt: . . . Suppose you talk it over with Perkins now. I think that perhaps to have Fall nominate me would emphasize what I would like to have emphasized, that if you want the antithesis of Wilson you want to take me.

Perkins then took the phone and gave Roosevelt a rundown on the results of his own canvassing among the Republican delegates.

Perkins: . . . Curiously enough we figure up 81 or 82 votes on the first ballot. . . . Now I have purposely tried to minimize the vote on the first ballot and have given out that we expect 70 or 75. . . . On the second ballot we know we will have more than 75 and then we will be in the running. . . . A good many are after me about your not being a Republican. I have made this suggestion to [Idaho's Senator William E.] Borah, for him to think over. . . . I said, "You want the Colonel and his party. Now suppose that I could get our people [the Progressives] to authorize me to say to you, confidentially, that provided the Colonel, the right Vice President and the platform were put up, we would immediately pick up our banners, walk down to the Coliseum and surrender, body, boots and breeches." Borah said, "That is some suggestion."

Roosevelt: George, that is a master stroke. It must have made a great impression.

 "I think Hughes a good deal of a skunk in the attitude he has taken."

Wednesday and Thursday, June 8 and 9 As the conventions opened the professionals of each party managed to maintain control of the convention machinery and to pave the way for compromise. Progressive William Draper Lewis met with Senator Lodge and together they drafted the party platforms. which were nearly identical. Party leaders also managed to engineer the appointment of a conference committee consisting of five Progressives and five Republicans. On Thursday evening Medill McCormick of Illinois, a pro-Roosevelt Republican, explained to the Colonel the composition of the Republican committee.

McCormick: . . . The Republican convention has just appointed a conference committee consisting of [Murray] Crane [of Massachusetts], Nicholas Murray Butler, ex-Congressman Johnson of Ohio, Borah and Reed Smoot. . . .

* *This was the same Albert Fall who, as Secretary of the Interior in the Harding Administration, became involved in the Teapot Dome oil-lease scandals and was forced to resign from the Cabinet. He was later tried and convicted in criminal court and sent to prison.*

In my delegation the tide today turned very strong for Hughes. For instance, some fellows who have been close friends of mine personally, although I have opposed them politically, have given me a private tip to get out of the way. . . .

Roosevelt: Now tell me, when do you think the nominations will come?

McCormick: The nominations will be made some time tomorrow. The Bull Moose [Progressive] crowd are now over in the auditorium, appointing their conference committee. . . .

Roosevelt: Of course I have never believed that there was a chance of my nomination and I have been very anxious that the thing should work out right for the country's best interest. Hughes has been a big disappointment thus far. I guess there is no need to tell you that I think Hughes a good deal of a skunk in the attitude he has taken.

While Roosevelt and McCormick were talking, the Progressives appointed their delegates to the conference committee. Perkins headed the group, which also consisted of Governor Hiram Johnson of California, Charles J. Bonaparte of Maryland, John M. Parker of Louisiana, and H. S. Wilkinson of New York.

Their first session with the Republicans, held at the Chicago Club, was orderly, congenial, frank—and fruitless. When the Progressives offered Roosevelt as a "compromise" candidate, Nicholas Murray Butler stated that "under no circumstances whatever would the Republican convention consent to his nomination." Perkins asked the Republicans to suggest someone else. This they refused to do, saying that they could not commit the convention to any man so early in the game. At 3:30 A.M. on Friday, June 9, the conferees adjourned, having accomplished nothing.

Friday, June 9

After learning of the failure of the meeting, the Republican convention proceeded to the nomination of candidates, a complicated, windy process which consumed most of Friday. Many Progressive delegates reacted by demanding that Roosevelt be selected at once, without regard for the Republicans. At 3:30 on Friday afternoon William Allen White of Kansas was on the private wire to Oyster Bay, asking Roosevelt's permission to go ahead with his nomination in the Progressive convention.

White: . . . We feel that we can go over a couple of ballots but that it would be a little dangerous to go further than that.

Roosevelt: I do not think we ought to nominate until they [the Republicans] have had a full chance. . . . You know I haven't committed myself in any way about running on a third ticket, but as you know I am very reluctant to do so.

White: Naturally.

Roosevelt: I can see that only damage would come from

Charles Evans Hughes

it. I think it would hurt to nominate me until they have acted. . . .

White: If the Republican convention does not show a decided tendency to come our way they [the Progressives] will nominate you pretty soon.

Roosevelt: Try to keep our convention from acting today. Keep them from acting until tomorrow. Let us see the drift of this evening and then call me up tomorrow. . . .

White: I think it can be very easily handled for tonight provided the Republicans do not go into session tonight and stampede for Hughes. Our people do not like the Hughes proposition.

Roosevelt: I do not like the Hughes proposition myself; I loathe it. I think Hughes is a man of the Wilson type; I think he is little better than Wilson. . . .

White: He must get out from under that German proposition before our people will consider him.

Yet White was a self-confessed leader of a group of "conspirators" who worked day and night to undermine Perkins' control of the convention and proceed at once to the nomination of Roosevelt. At 8 P.M. Perkins reported to Roosevelt.

Perkins: We have had an extraordinary day here. . . . I really feel hopeful tonight for the first time. . . .

Roosevelt: George, I should like to be where I could hold your hand. . . . Did White tell you what he came down to tell me? He came to tell me that he had consulted with . . . the conservative side of the Progressive party, and said that they had decided that they were willing to yield to my wishes to the extent of waiting for one ballot. They wanted to know if I wished to be nominated after the first, or whether they should wait until after the second.

Perkins: When I got back to the convention I found they had it all framed up to nominate you, and [Raymond] Robins [chairman of the convention] told me that they did not propose to listen to any more nonsense about postponing your nomination and were going to put you through.

Roosevelt: George, there is no doubt about it; the other fellows have all the crooks and we have all the cranks.

(**Note from Mary Kihm:** I was called away at this point and did not get back to the telephone until the following remark by Colonel Roosevelt.)

Roosevelt: However, much as I despise Hughes I would prefer him to one of the burglars [i.e., those who had "stolen" the nomination from him in 1912—Ed.]. Even the members of our lunatic fringe take that view.

Twenty minutes later Roosevelt was getting a report on the Republican convention from John W. McGrath, Roosevelt's private secretary, and Dr. Edward A. Rumely, owner of the New York Evening Mail.

McGrath: They have gone to ballot in the other convention but we haven't heard anything from it as yet.

Roosevelt: Oh, Mac, go get your gun!

Rumely: I was at the Republican convention when you were nominated. The reporters said it was the first live demonstration. . . . Hughes was cheered for twenty minutes but it was a weak, thin thing. Joe Cannon and Harding looked down from one side of the platform and then down the other to see what was doing. Here's the proposition: They are a very astute bunch of poker players. I watch the delegates. I talked with one Massachusetts delegate, Patch, who is known not to favor you. He stood up on a chair and I said, "What are you up for?" and he said, "I'm for Roosevelt but I haven't been able to say it until now." There are others like him, but here's the situation: If they come to a vote and are only guessing whether or not there is a third party in the field they are very likely to follow their leaders; but if they know there is a third party in the field they will be afraid not to endorse you. . . .

Gifford Pinchot, pioneer conservationist and one of Roosevelt's closest friends and staunchest Progressive supporters, was then put on the line.

Pinchot: Our weakness here from the start, as indicated in my letter to you, remains the same—the doubt on the part of your opponents as to what you will do in case of your nomination by the Progressives; in other words, the feeling has got around among them, from somewhere or other, that if you are nominated and they had anyone that is even approximately bearable, you would withdraw and their nomination would stand. That is what has made us weak in dealing with them. We have been playing poker with them substantially without chips in that direction. Now I realize,

of course, the difficulty of that situation; at the same time, if you could send to some one here a telegram or a message over the telephone which could be circulated and which, without directly committing you finally to make the race, would indicate that that was your intention, and that could become known to the other side, it would very much strengthen our case.

Roosevelt: . . . I do not believe that good would come from such a communication as you suggest. . . .

White and the other "radicals" were unable to get control of the Progressive convention on Friday. Over at the Coliseum, the Republicans wound up their oratory and began to vote. The first ballot was a great disappointment to the friends of Roosevelt in both conventions. Hughes had an impressive lead over the field, whereas Roosevelt was far down the list of candidates with only 65 votes. The second ballot greatly increased Hughes's lead and added only a handful of new supporters to Roosevelt's candidacy. At this point the nomination of Hughes seemed inevitable unless a deal with the Progressives could be arranged. The Republican leaders therefore adjourned the session to allow for a final effort at compromise.

The results of the first two ballots had demonstrated clearly that Roosevelt could not win the Republican nomination. For Roosevelt, this practically settled the question of his own action. So long as he had hopes of a double nomination he was willing to consider the possibility of running independently, should the Republicans make an objectionable choice; without those hopes the possibility disappeared.

Fearing just this development, some of the Progressives attempted to force Roosevelt's hand.

 "I am not going to dictate to that convention as if I were a Tammany chieftain."

Pinchot: Have you heard the result of the first ballot?

Roosevelt: Yes, I got [65], did I not? The Republicans must [realize] that if they carry things too far they may make it absolutely necessary for me to run on a third ticket but I absolutely will not commit myself in advance. I wish you would look around and see who else would run; see Hiram Johnson.

Pinchot: He will not. As things stand tonight I do not see how it is possible for anything of that sort to happen, and your refusal to run would kill the Progressive party entirely. That seems to be self-evident. . . .

Roosevelt: I wish to say this—that there is a very wide difference between making a young colonel and a retired major general lead a forlorn hope. I have simply got to reserve judgment.

Pinchot: There is one thing I want to say. There is apparently throughout the convention a very strong fear that if we wait until after the Republicans have nominated, and if they nominate Hughes, an effort will be made at that time to force our convention to nominate Hughes.

Roosevelt: I do not see how. I can only say for myself: If the Republican convention now nominated Hughes I would have to say that even though the Progressives endorsed him I would not endorse him until he repudiated the German-American alliance.

Pinchot: I want you to make it evident that our people will nominate you; then you decide afterwards what to do.

Roosevelt: Now see here; that is a big order.

Pinchot: I do not want you to make a public statement but I want you to make it evident to your managers here that you do not want anyone to take steps to have our convention nominate Hughes.

Roosevelt: I'll take those steps.

Pinchot: There is a very strong fear among men whose judgment is to be respected that an effort of that kind will be made.

Roosevelt: Now I'll tell you, Gifford, I have purposely arranged that I would tell everything to Hiram Johnson and George Perkins. . . . Now you consult Hiram Johnson.

Pinchot: Now will you tell George Perkins the same thing? You cannot expect our convention to wait until Hughes makes a statement. We have got to act before that happens. You cannot keep our people here a week.

Roosevelt: Now, Gifford, take that up with Hiram Johnson and Perkins and have them make some suggestions to me.

Pinchot: All you have to do, Theodore, is to let your will be known to your managers.

Roosevelt: My will known to the managers? I am not going to dictate to that convention as if I were a Tammany chieftain. That is just what I want to avoid doing.

Pinchot: There is no question of your dictating. The convention wants to do only one thing and is afraid that plans are being put in operation to prevent it from doing so, and I want you to make it plain that those plans have not your approval, if they exist.

Roosevelt: Very good; now you mean that plans are being put in existence to secure the endorsement of Hughes if he is nominated—the endorsement of Hughes before he has made any statement. Now then, I personally will not support Hughes until I know where he stands.

Pinchot: May I quote you as to that?

Roosevelt: Yes, but you must not quote me to the newspapers.

Pinchot: Well, then, whom can I quote you to?

Roosevelt: What do you mean? Do you mean to say that you think you can quote me to the newspapers? Of course you cannot. Quote me to Hiram Johnson, to William Allen White, to Henry Allen, to George Perkins.

Pinchot: Dr. Rumely wants to speak to you for one moment.

Roosevelt: O, for the Lord's sake! All right.

Rumely: They are having difficulty in keeping the Progressive convention from nominating you. Johnson is holding the floor now. He is saying that for two days he has been part of a strategy he did not believe in; that it is only your will that has kept him from going through with the plan he thought should be put through. If you could realize the situation in Chicago you would feel you have a much stronger hand than I think you now feel you have.

Roosevelt: I have told Hiram Johnson and I have told George Perkins that they must be in consultation. Let Hiram Johnson and George Perkins get together, and if they differ then let them come to me.

At 10:30 P.M. George B. Cortelyou, Roosevelt's former secretary, was on the wire, speaking to Roosevelt about the meeting—then just getting under way at the Chicago Club—of the Progressive-Republican conference committee.

Cortelyou: . . . G. W. [Perkins] asked what I thought they should do when they went into this conference committee tonight. Neither convention can push the thing to a conclusion until the conference committee reports back that their efforts have been unavailing; any other course would be a slap in the face of the convention. They cannot go on forever. I should think that tonight there ought to be a showdown. . . . I should imagine G. W. would have to be guided somewhat by the statement made to him by the Republican conferees as to the line he will take. Of course he feels now that he has about got to the point where he cannot hold that Progressive crowd much longer. They meet at 10:30 tomorrow—a half hour before the other one—so that they will get into action right away unless they are controlled and unless this conference committee has something to say.

*"Now, George, it's hard
to know what is best to do.
What is your judgment?"*

Roosevelt: My judgment is that the conference committee cannot say anything. They will have to say that they disagreed.

Cortelyou: The next question comes up after the action of the Progressive convention tomorrow. If they nominate you at once, then comes the question of whether they should complete the ticket or hold over a while to see what effect the first nomination will have.

Roosevelt: Now, George, it's hard to know what is best to do. If they nominate me shall I take a little time to decide? Should I take two or three hours to consider it? What is your judgment?

Cortelyou: I should think so, because if they nominate at once that would be before the other convention opened. You could accept it at once, but from our point of view that would look as though you wanted to take snap judgment.

Roosevelt: But, my dear boy, I do not intend to accept.

Cortelyou: I know, but in talking with the conference

committee tonight I imagine **G. W.** cannot show his hand on that.

The difficulty Roosevelt now faced was this: If he were to oppose Hughes, whom could he suggest (other than himself) as an alternative? As the conference committee met again in another attempt to find a common candidate, everyone realized that this was the last chance for the "bosses" to exert the control they liked to think they possessed. If they could not agree, the separate nominations of Roosevelt and Hughes would surely follow in the morning.

But agree they could not. The Progressives still insisted they had no name to offer but Roosevelt's; the Republicans rejected him, but would suggest no one else.

Shortly before 3 A.M. the committee adjourned. But as the weary conferees were leaving the club, Perkins asked Nicholas Murray Butler if he would be willing to talk to Roosevelt on the private wire. Butler asked for time to discuss this idea with some of his friends, and after they had agreed he hurried to Perkins' room at the Blackstone. Perkins got Roosevelt on the phone at ten minutes to three.

Perkins: I must talk very quickly and then will put Nicholas Murray Butler on the telephone in a minute. All I want to be sure to do is to tell you that you must not say in any way that you are for this man, that man or the other. . . . He will try hard to see if you personally will stand for [Elihu] Root, [Charles W.] Fairbanks or some one of that sort. . . .

Roosevelt: What is the use of it?

Perkins: I don't know. This is all along the line of trading out before morning. . . .

Roosevelt: Hello; this is Colonel Roosevelt.

Butler: Hello; this is Murray Butler.

Roosevelt: How do you do, President of Columbia College?

Butler: We have been having a very interesting time out here. . . . Now the situation in the Republican party is just this: The so-called [here Miss Kihm missed a phrase—probably "favorite sons"—Ed.] cannot hold their vote from Hughes much longer. The outlook now is that Hughes will be nominated on the first or second ballot in the morning. That is to me and a great many of us a desperate calamity. The fact of the matter, whether Mr. Hughes knows it or not, is that all the pussyfooters and pro-Germans in Chicago are for him, and that of itself has excited my suspicion.

Roosevelt: And he is not going to make any statement until after his nomination?

Butler: No, and then it will be futile. . . . Now I regard it as impossible to elect him, no matter who endorses him. I regard it as assuring four more years of this awful Wilson. I am most anxious—and I have a great many of our people in condition to talk sense—to find some way, if possible, to prevent Hughes's nomination, and there is only one way to prevent it, and that is to say to them that someone has

been found who is satisfactory to the Progressives and who has your support. . . .

Butler then made three suggestions: Elihu Root, Charles W. Fairbanks, who had been Roosevelt's Vice President and a senator from Indiana, and Philander C. Knox, a veteran of the Senate and of Cabinet posts. Of these Root was clearly the largest figure both in intellect and in experience, having served in the Senate and as secretary of state and of war. But he was over 65, and he was particularly hated by the Progressives for his cynical smothering of the Roosevelt forces in the 1912 Republican convention. Both Butler and Roosevelt realized he was hopeless as a compromise candidate. The others, lesser men, received serious consideration.

"Mexico is our Balkan Peninsula and we will have to deal with it."

Butler: There is some talk of Fairbanks, whose record I am not familiar with but whose record with you I do know about. And then there is Knox, who has been little mentioned here.

Roosevelt: Let me interrupt with a word about Knox. I am devoted to Knox personally, but unfortunately he is just as responsible for this Mexican situation as the present Administration. [Roosevelt felt that Knox, as Taft's secretary of state, had been partially responsible for what Roosevelt considered the mishandling of the Mexican Revolution.—Ed.] . . . After peace the submarine episodes will be but a memory, but Mexico is our Balkan peninsula and we will have to handle it; and we will be met at every step in our condemnation of Wilson with what our candidate himself has done. Lodge will tell you that too.

Butler: What is there to be said in a general way about Fairbanks?

Roosevelt: . . . I really have a real liking for Fairbanks personally. He is to me a very much better man than Hughes, but I am horribly afraid that he will prove impossible to do anything with. . . . I need not tell you that I am in the same position you are. I have to get the Progressive convention to agree in the same way that you must get the Republican convention in agreement. Fairbanks I personally would like. . . . Would there be any chance of taking up an entirely new man?

Butler: I think it possible, although it might surprise them very much.

Roosevelt: . . . Now would there be a chance of taking up Leonard Wood?

Butler: I don't think there would be, for this reason: There would not be any objection to him personally, but it would not meet with the approval of the western and southwestern states. . . . In view of our preparedness program they would not approve of a military man. . . .

Roosevelt: Of course he would understand very speedily that the tariff and such matters were entirely outside his realm and would get on the Army and Navy question and Americanism at once. He wouldn't have to do as Brother Hughes will have to do—improvise. Would there be any possibility of putting Lodge across?

Butler: . . . I don't know what vote-getting qualities Lodge has.

Roosevelt: I don't myself; but he has the political habit and these men would get on with him. . . .

Butler: Suppose I have a talk with Perkins along the lines we have been talking? . . . Will you just hold the wire and I'll get Perkins? Sorry to have got you out of bed at this hour.

Roosevelt: Heavens and earth, man, don't speak of it. Look what you must have been doing all these nights while I have been lolling around doing nothing.

"I know Lodge's record like a book. He is just as straight as a string."

Roosevelt then reported to Perkins the main points of his conversation with Butler. Perkins rang off to confer with Butler, to whom he proposed the following plan: The Progressive leaders (presumably in Roosevelt's name) would draft a statement refusing to support Hughes. This statement could be pushed through the Progressive convention, however, only by coupling it with the nomination of Roosevelt, which the great mass of the delegates was hot to accomplish. After that the Progressives would adjourn, sending their anti-Hughes statement to the Republicans. Then the Republicans would have no choice but to accept Roosevelt if they wanted to win the election. "I want it distinctly understood," Perkins told Butler in explaining his scheme, "that if we do that you are going to say to your friends that it was we who saved them [from Hughes] and that you are not going to hold it up against us for nominating our man first." At 3:30 Butler left to confer with the other Republicans on the compromise committee, promising to let Perkins know before dawn if this course of action seemed feasible. Perkins called Roosevelt back and outlined the new plan.

Roosevelt: That is one of the most extraordinary things I have ever heard. I want to say right here, although you may not agree with me, that I am sure I was right in speaking of Wood and Lodge.

Perkins: I am sorry you mentioned Lodge. We are in the position, as it stands now, of not submitting any choice to those people except you. That is perfectly all right because they have never submitted anyone to us. . . . Still, I don't

like our record. Somebody might say that you should have suggested someone else. . . . [Yet Lodge] is the only man familiar with the international situation and one who could be agreed on by both conventions. Is there anything you can think of in Lodge's record that would be against that proposition?

Roosevelt: I know Lodge's record like a book. There has never been anything against it at any time, except, of course, George, that he does not have as advanced views as you and I.

Perkins: I think we could take care of that.

Roosevelt: We have, first of all, to deal with preparedness and Americanism, because they are questions of internal relations. Then foreign relations. [Lodge] is chairman of the Foreign Relations Committee. He is just as straight as a string. Do you want me to talk to Hiram Johnson?

Perkins: Not on your life; not for an hour or two.

Roosevelt: Then I won't say a word. I want to add this, if you will, George. Keep Hiram Johnson in touch with me so he won't fly off the handle and think I am neglecting him.

Perkins: Of course I'll do that, but at the right moment. . . . I think it was a very grave mistake to suggest Wood. He is not acceptable to anybody. He is a military man. It puts you in a bad light.

Roosevelt: It has been rejected and I will not follow it up at all. I am glad you have come to the conclusion to suggest Lodge. Fortunately, Lodge has voted for me on the second ballot, so that we can use that with our wild-eyed Progressive friends.

Perkins: I may want to call you up in the morning and get a statement from you giving your reasons why you support Lodge.

Roosevelt: From now on I will not go to bed.

Perkins: All right, I will call you pretty often.

Saturday, June 10

Butler evidently got an unfavorable response to Perkins' suggestion from his Republican colleagues, for he makes no mention of it in his memoirs and there is no further record of it in the transcript of the telephone conversations. The Republican members of the conference committee decided finally that Hughes could not be stopped and, making the best of the situation, agreed to present his name to the joint committee as their "compromise" candidate.

In the meantime Roosevelt worked on a message to the two conventions suggesting Lodge's name, while Perkins routed the Senator from his bed and got him to agree to accept if chosen. At a quarter to nine on Saturday morning Perkins was again on the phone with Roosevelt. The Colonel offered to come to Chicago to argue on behalf of Lodge if the nominations could be postponed until Monday, but that was clearly impossible.

When the compromise committee met again, the

Republicans offered Hughes as their choice. The three Progressives (Hiram Johnson and John M. Parker had dropped out in disgust when they learned that Roosevelt wanted them to support the conservative Lodge) excused themselves to think this over. Ruefully, Perkins called Oyster Bay.

Roosevelt: Now, did you read my letter [recommending Lodge] to them?

Perkins: In view of this I do not think we should deliver that. . . .

Roosevelt: Well, George, I am awfully sorry about that. . . . Of course I am not going to accept Mr. Hughes, and I am going to ask you to put my letter before that committee.

Perkins: . . . You understand, of course, that Johnson and Parker will not stand for the counter-proposition, so we will just turn it in as the major report of our committee, submitted to you. Perhaps we might just as well put it in as coming from you and not as coming from the committee.

Roosevelt: Put it right in as from me, that's right.

Several Progressives urged Roosevelt to reconsider his decision about the Lodge letter. One of these was Walter Brown, a conservative member of the Progressive National Committee.

Brown: Mr. Perkins wanted me to ask you if you had considered the fact that that letter would probably eliminate you from any further chance in that convention.

Roosevelt: . . . I have passed that stage. I have considered everything in connection with it. I wish that letter presented at once. . . .

Perkins himself made one last effort to bend the strong Roosevelt will.

Perkins: There are five or six of us here, discussing this situation. [We] feel that . . . it would be better not to turn in the Lodge letter now.

Roosevelt: I disagree with you. I considered that whole thing when I wrote that letter. I must request you definitely and at once to put that letter before the conferees.

Against such a positive command no one could argue. Wearily, and with profound misgivings, Perkins ar-

ranged for the statement to be read to the two conventions. While he was doing so Roosevelt talked again with some of his more radical supporters. To former Governor Robert Bass of New Hampshire he explained his position with special clearness.

Roosevelt: I do not ask our people to accept one of the burglars. I do not ask them to accept any man who isn't of the highest character and who does not stand absolutely square on the issues of today. I think Hughes has shown himself in the most contemptible possible light, and so I am not now asking any of our people to support him; that must be determined by events; but I do feel that if the Republicans are willing to do what I have asked, the Progressives should join with them. . . .

Bass: I believe the Republicans will nominate Hughes. We cannot accept a man whose position is totally unknown to us, and the only thing we can do is to place our nomination in your hands, to be held in trust and to do with as you see fit and in accordance with the things we have stood for.

Roosevelt: Well, Bob . . . you are proposing to put a very, very heavy burden on me. . . . We have got to see what the Progressive and Republican conventions do with my communication. . . .

The conventions acted as everyone but Roosevelt had expected they would act. When Perkins addressed the Progressives, his speech was continually interrupted by hoots and catcalls, and at his presentation of the names of Hughes and Lodge, "loud agonizing No's echoed through the hall." The Republicans listened phlegmatically to the reading of Roosevelt's suggestion and then proceeded to give Hughes the nomination at once, and unanimously at that. As soon as word of this reached the Progressives, they simply swept the protesting Perkins out of the way and nominated Roosevelt by acclamation.

This nomination was completed at 12:37 on Saturday afternoon. Less than ten minutes later the leaders were talking to Roosevelt again on the private wire. Different points of view were presented to him as to what he should do about the nomination, but it was

Roosevelt himself, speaking to Perkins, who made the decision.

Roosevelt: George, we have got to have our skirts absolutely clear. . . . And here is my thought: that I should answer them [the Progressive delegates] that if they wish a definite answer now I must refuse to accept and must ask them to nominate someone else; however, if they wish, and only if they wish, I am content to act as follows: that is, to turn over to the National Committee my conditional refusal to accept the nomination and run on a third ticket until the committee has had an opportunity to find out where Hughes stands. . . . Then, if the National Committee thinks Hughes's attitude is entirely satisfactory, they can so announce and no further action on my declination will be taken.

Perkins agreed and Roosevelt rang off to prepare a statement along these lines. While various drafts of his statement were being formulated and revised, he continued to talk with important Progressive delegates throughout the afternoon. Among them was his son.

Theodore, Jr.: Hello, father.
Roosevelt: Hello, my son.
Theodore, Jr.: In the first place, in connection with that statement of yours, I think we want to be particularly careful, if we are going to support Hughes as we probably will, that we say nothing that will reflect on him in our statements here. . . . The statement reads as if you did not approve of Hughes. You don't, of course.
Roosevelt: Of course I will support him, but I will not be responsible for him.

Later Roosevelt talked with Hiram Johnson. The terrible-tempered fire-eater now seemed resigned to Roosevelt's withdrawing in favor of Hughes.

Johnson: Hello, Colonel.
Roosevelt: How is the Honorable Hiram? . . . Are you in a pliable and compromising mood?
Johnson: . . . I feel this way, Colonel. I feel that the thing is coming to the point where you have to quit the nomination. I would really prefer to perform the operation today and not have you bothered and troubled. . . .
Roosevelt: My own feeling is just as you said a year ago —that I will go fishing; you said that you anticipated that in this campaign you and I would like to go fishing. I think my fishing trip has begun. If you will remember, you said then that it was not right to ask me to run and you did not regard it as right to ask you to run.
Johnson: I felt that way then and feel that way now. I think it would be a crime to ask you to run unless there is some great national thing that demands it.

* * *

The rest of the story is anticlimactic. Hughes's statements proved satisfactory to a majority of the Progressive National Committee, and on June 26 they voted to support him. Roosevelt had already made up his own mind, and on June 28 he dined with the candidate, formally making his peace. Hughes, of course, was beaten by Wilson in a close race, featured by Hughes's loss of California because of a misunderstanding with the influential Hiram Johnson.

The chief result of the dramatic developments of the two conventions was the utter destruction of the Progressive party. Its chief undertaker was Theodore Roosevelt. Had he so willed, it would have gone on, to defeat no doubt in 1916, but to no one knows what future developments. As it was, its members either returned with Roosevelt to the Republican camp or switched to Woodrow Wilson and the Democrats.

No doubt some of Roosevelt's supporters thought him a traitor. It is true that he and men like Perkins made cynical use of the Progressive convention, treating it, as Professor George Mowry has said, "as a stalking horse and a trading horse." But Roosevelt was utterly convinced that Wilson, because of his neutralism in the European war, had to be defeated if the national honor were to be preserved. And, if Roosevelt wanted the nomination himself at the beginning of the conventions, no one can deny that at the end he made a serious and unselfish effort to find a satisfactory compromise between himself and Hughes. His judgment in pushing Lodge was faulty, but his motive was neither insincere, nor corrupt, nor selfish. Nor did he at any time try to deceive those of his supporters who wanted him to run as a Progressive.

History may judge his actions to have been misguided, foolish, even tragic, when one considers that the destruction of the Progressive party made the Republican party a stronghold of super-conservatism for at least a generation. But history has the benefit of hindsight. Things might well have worked out differently. Had Roosevelt not died in 1919 he would almost certainly have been the Republican candidate in 1920, for by supporting Hughes he had rehabilitated himself with the party regulars. He would have won in 1920, and at the very least, the nation would have been spared the sorry antics of the Harding Administration. In any case, this much is beyond argument: throughout the battle of 1916 Roosevelt did what he thought was in the best interests of the nation and of those principles in which he sincerely believed.

John A. Garraty of Michigan State's history faculty has written biographies of several statesmen of the Roosevelt era. This is his fifth article in AMERICAN HERITAGE, *the most recent being "A Lion in the Street" last June.*

READING, WRITING, AND HISTORY

By BRUCE CATTON

Half-Horse, Half-Alligator

Central to the American experience is the fact that in this land men have had to create their own traditions. Out of a past still too close to be fully understood have come legends which turn into articles of faith before they are even complete. And no article of faith has had greater force with us than the one which centers about the era of the great frontier and its part in forming the American character.

The precise formulation of this article of faith was probably best undertaken by Frederick Jackson Turner, who saw the distinctive quality of American character and institutions as deriving from the frontier experience. What we believe in, do, and are, Turner suggested, can be understood only with reference to the western experience, which has been much more important than any heritage we have from European culture. Indeed, Turner saw American democracy itself as coming "stark and strong and full of life, from the American forest."

Recent historians have found many faults with Turner's thesis, but that he expressed what a great many of his fellow citizens devoutly believe is undeniable. No American legend has been stronger than the one which finds great virtues and a powerful faith centering about the heroic pioneer. Somehow, we feel, natural man himself came into his own on the frontier—untaught and unvarnished, and with many rough edges, but grandly free from the accumulated errors and constricting shibboleths of the Old World. Under everything else, natural man was *good,* and his goodness abides with us to this day.

Upon this belief Arthur K. Moore casts a skeptical eye in a stimulating new book, *The Frontier Mind,* which is less a discussion of the Turner thesis than it is an examination of exactly what went on in one particular part of the legendary frontier, the state of Kentucky. Here, he suggests, the whole frontier tradition has its base; from Kentucky, according to the books, the pioneer bravely and with much vision stepped off toward the Pacific; in Kentucky he built a culture which was both peculiarly American and extremely successful. During the formative period, Kentucky *was* the frontier. Put it under the microscope and what do you see?

What Mr. Moore sees is not exactly in line with the grand tradition, and he suggests that the reality and

---

The Frontier Mind: a Cultural Analysis of the Kentucky Frontiersman, by Arthur K. Moore. University of Kentucky Press; 264 pp. $5.00.

---

the myth began to part company at a fairly early stage. Yet the myth, somehow, was fated, almost as if the belief in the virtues of frontier life antedated the frontier experience itself. For among men of European heritage, as Mr. Moore points out, there existed, generations ago, a millennial belief in an attainable earthly paradise, and this obviously was going to be found, if anywhere, in the American West; specifically, late in the eighteenth century, in Kentucky.

Moving to the frontier, thus, the settler anticipated something like a paradisaical existence—which, among other things, meant a life without any particular restraints; and among people touched by this illusion, Mr. Moore remarks, "a keen sense of social responsibility is not to be expected." Personal freedom and physical satisfaction are expected, and frequently attained, but the primitive masculine virtues are exalted and there is created a society "mature enough to plan and execute but not to reflect." The epic Indian-fighter and forest-tamer of legend can look a good deal more attractive at a distance than at close range.

Thus Kentucky had not advanced far along the road toward full settlement before it had created that legendary character, the "half-horse, half-alligator" rough-and-tumble fighter embodied in scores of myths. Grotesque caricature though he was, this horse-alligator did embody the cult of primitivism at its worst. The antithesis of civilized man, he nevertheless represented something civilized man had in him; the literary tradition might transform him into a Daniel Boone or a Deerslayer, who has scant use for civilization but nevertheless stands as an agent of progress, but he continues to speak for an anarchic tendency in the mind of the well-tamed inhabitant of the city.

What Mr. Moore is getting at here, clearly enough, is a deep-seated cleavage in the American mind. For much more than a century we have been developing an urbanized society in America, yet somehow we have always had our doubts. And we have from the beginning turned to the frontiersman as a type figure to prove to our dissatisfied subconscious that natural goodness, natural law, and natural humanity, untouched by the restraints and teachings of a tightly-knit society, are good and proper guidelines for our faith and conduct. The noble savage of frontier society, transplanted into a culture whose frontier has long since evaporated, may be a defective guide for a people undertaking to make moral judgments; in such case, says Mr. Moore, the noble savage "understandably loses much of his protective coloration and reveals lineaments of the alligator-horse, another name for unshirted barbarism."

We retain, in other words, even in a highly complex society, a large trace of the frontier mind; that is, a determination to preserve both unprecedented liberty and a curious social and intellectual innocence. On the actual frontier this was all very well, but what comes down from it is an attitude of doubtful usefulness since it implies a rejection of the responsibilities that go with civilization. The frontier legend, Mr. Moore believes, brings with it a general opposition to "programs implying discipline and discrimination." Implicit in all of this is a severing of old cultural ties.

Men whose whole concern is with the future have little use for the lessons and experience of the past, and a magnificent broadening of the physical horizon was not necessarily accompanied by a corresponding broadening of intellectual horizons.

For a summing up, Mr. Moore offers the following:

"What seriously occupied the mind of the West during the nineteenth century was not then intellectual or even spiritual values but the tariff, public lands, internal improvements, Indian affairs, and markets. Rugged and self-reliant individualists by reputation, westerners from Kentucky to the Pacific yet assumed that the national government had a special obligation to help them with the garden, and at the polls they regularly underscored their assumption. Since the garden yielded magnificently, life was abundant in material things; and the conclusion could hardly be resisted that prosperity was the truest measure of well-being. With riches came a sense of power and importance and a desire to win the world's approval. Radically affected by the garden psychology, the West could not fully realize that wealth was only one of several criteria by which the rest of the world judged cultures."

Obsessed by the frontier, did we indeed become so interested in what lay ahead of us that we let our old culture languish without evolving a proper substitute? Several kinds of romantic desiring were brought together on the frontier, but the more heroic and noble elements tended to fade as the frontier itself remained; what is left, Mr. Moore suggests, is all too often the lawless and unrestrained image of the horse-alligator, "confronting the metropolis with the image of its own dark unconscious mind."

Frontier in the City

All of this is very perceptive, as far as it goes; yet it should be remarked that there has been an urban frontier in this country, as well as a frontier pitched on the thin edge of the trackless forests and the untamed rivers, and the same forces do seem to have been at work on it. Kentucky may have sent the horse-alligator down to give us unquiet nights, but a reasonable facsimile of this creature was born and nourished in the American city as well, and for proof of it you might pay a little attention to a rather shocking book called *July, 1863*, by Irving Werstein.

What Mr. Werstein has to offer could be either a final chapter or an article in rebuttal to Mr. Moore's book: a study of the five dreadful days of murder, arson, and general lawlessness which descended on New York City a few days after the Battle of Gettysburg as a result of the Federal government's attempt to enforce a military conscription law. The word "incredible" in the book's subtitle is well chosen, for this ugly little chapter in American history goes almost beyond belief.

On the surface, what happened in New York then was the direct result of the fantastic stupidity and timorousness with which the Lincoln Administration in the Civil War approached the matter of conscription. By 1863 the government was ready to admit that it must compel certain citizens to enter the Army, which until then had been composed entirely of volunteers. It was afraid to grapple with the problem in a forthright way, however, and—in an unconscionably inept

---

July, 1863: the Incredible Story of the Bloody New York City Draft Riots, by Irving Werstein. Julian Messner, Inc.; 252 pp. $3.95.

---

effort to sugar-coat the pill—it devised a draft which could be avoided by any draftee who was able to pay a $300 commutation fee, which automatically meant that the wage earner had to carry the load. The government then undertook to enforce this law in the city of New York, which was full of a rootless proletariat which, because of corrupt municipal misgovernment and a vicious national display of antiforeignism, had become fully predisposed to violent action. Unhappily enough, this action came precisely when irresponsible politicians were teaching that the Civil War itself was being fought solely for the purpose of ending Negro slavery; the freed slaves, it was argued, would infallibly flock to the city and there would undermine a labor market which was already in a very disturbed condition.

With a bad law bearing down on a city crowd which had never been told that anyone in America was prepared to do anything but exploit it, the result—quite naturally—was an explosion. Stimulated, apparently, to some extent by Confederate agents, but owing its real explosive force to the country's abject failure to assimilate the floods of workers who were coming in from Europe, the mob struck back with primitive fury. It broke up the conscription centers, battled the police, engaged in a vicious race war, looted shops and homes, and loosed on the city five days of actual warfare which ended only when veterans from the Army of the Potomac moved in with shotted guns to restore order. To this day no one knows, within several hundred, the total number of people who were killed.

Mr. Werstein's book is vivid, though somewhat confusing; his fondness for inventing conversations and for "dramatizing" incidents which, Heaven knows, might be supposed to carry their own dramatic values

built in, leaves one hard put now and then to know where actual history stops and touched-up history begins. But it would be hard to overstate the horror of the draft riots very much, and for the most part this book gives a faithful picture of the occasion. It is a picture whose grim significance speaks for itself.

For it becomes clear, reading this one on the heels of Mr. Moore's book, that the urban frontier in America had its own horse-alligator thesis, arising for much the same reason as Kentucky's. America was being built from scratch, and the hundreds of thousands of immigrants who survived the miseries of the steerage in order to set foot on the New World at the mouth of the Hudson believed, as much as the western pioneers ever believed it, that they were somehow approaching a Garden of Eden where all things would work out for their good. They got into a jungle, fully as dark and menacing as anything the Kentucky frontier ever had to offer, and they needed to have the same care for their scalps; the environment taught them that only the primitive virtues counted for much, and when the pressure of an enormous civil war came down on them, loaded with intangibles that are hard enough to see even at a century's distance, they acted about as one might expect. The draft riots were the hideous result.

The horse-alligator, in short, is there, deep in the subconscious, in the city as well as in the country. It may be that this nation was built up too fast, and that certain values were ignored in the building. Whatever the answer, a critical re-examination of the way in which it all happened is very much in order. Two more different books than these by Mr. Moore and Mr. Werstein could not easily be imagined, yet in the end they teach very much the same lesson.

FROM *Frank Leslie's Illustrated Newspaper,* 1863

The Boz Ball CONTINUED FROM PAGE 11

Another observer, reminiscing many years later, described the arrival of Dickens at the ball:

I remember the immense crowd of the "beauty and fashion" of New York that filled the theatre from its dancing floor, laid over stage and pit, to the gallery. . . . I think Irving and Cooper were there—I am sure of Halleck and Bryant. . . . There was a rush near the door, a flutter through the crowded theatre, a hush of expectation, a burst of "See the Conquering Hero Comes," and the author of Pickwick and the Uncommercial Traveller, with all of the humor and pathos that lie between, burst upon our astonished and delighted vision. Then the cheers, then the waving of handkerchiefs from floor to boxes, and all the tiers—and tears, no doubt, of joy and happiness, and bouquets innumerable gave what was possible to the irrepressible enthusiasm of the hour.

Newspapers throughout the country, even to the Mississippi frontier, carried ecstatic descriptions of the Boz Ball, exhausting all the adjectives in circulation at the time. The gowns and appearance of the loveliest belles of New York were described in detail. Mrs. Dickens wore "a white, figured Irish tabinet trimmed with mazarine blue flowers; a wreath of the same colour round her head, and with pearl necklace and earrings," while Dickens was described as "dressed in a suit of black, with a gay vest." One reporter noted with satisfaction that "the gentlemen and ladies were, of course, the middle and the richer classes of society, the price of tickets being such as to prevent a promiscuous attendance."

All in all, the Boz Ball was a great success, except in the opinion of a disgruntled few who were annoyed at being unable to obtain tickets and of a more numerous group who disapproved of what they considered wholly undignified, if not scandalous, proceedings. A minor fire had broken out during the ball but was quickly extinguished. A New York newspaper made the event an opportunity to sermonize on the evils of dancing and riotous behavior, asking, "What if the Theatre had been consumed with the *three thousand* dancers within its decorated walls? Were they not all prepared to die, and would it not have been a brilliant death-scene; a fitting close to the gay life they led?" The editorial concluded with the admonition: "Death is there. He haunts such places, and the steps of those who frequent them take hold on hell."

The event, however, that was to dull the brilliance of the Boz Ball irrevocably in the memories of many Americans—and of Dickens himself—took place after the ball was over. The managers of the Park Theatre, quick to recognize the bonanza within their doors, decided to put on a repeat performance at half the original price. Everything was to be the same as on the original night, including the presence of the British lion and his lioness. When the night arrived, Dickens was ill with a sore throat and declined the invitation to be honored a second time at half price. Appalled at the prospect of irate cash customers, the managers sent round to Dickens for a certificate to be signed by his physician testifying that he was unable to appear at the ball. Dickens was outraged at the boorish request, and the event may have provoked his decision to refuse any more invitations to public receptions in his honor, a decision which caused much resentment in the American cities he later visited. The episode undoubtedly contributed to his lampoon of such receptions in the pages of *Martin Chuzzlewit*, the novel he wrote upon his return to England, in which he recorded the most unpleasant of his American experiences and impressions.

A large portion of the American public shared Dickens' resentment of the action taken by the managers of the Park Theatre. A Boston paper remarked sarcastically that since he drew so well the managers should engage Boz for six or seven nights, adding, "We think this repetition turns the whole affair into a ridiculous burlesque—converting an act of courtesy to a private gentleman into a raree-show." Another editor commented, "The repetition of the Boz Ball in New York must, we think, induce Mr. Dickens to decline similar marks of attendance during the remainder of his stay in the country. We should like to see him received by the intelligent in a manner which his talents and goodness of heart render him worthy, but this attempt to make money by converting him into a mere show is detestable."

A number of Americans began to doubt the propriety of the whole tendency and character of the reception given to Dickens and asked whether there were not better ways of honoring a distinguished English author. Some even pointed out the irony of honoring Dickens with one hand while picking his pocket with the other and suggested that the passage of a long-overdue international copyright bill, aimed at the crushing of the American "bookaneers" (as Thomas Hood called them), would be the kind of tribute that would bring credit to the nation and genuine honor to Dickens. Though this suggestion went unheeded, other voices were raised in protest against the nature of the American welcome of Boz. In an editorial headed "More Bozziana" a Philadelphia paper had noted, just before the ball, that the names of the committee members appeared side by side with a list of applicants

This pencil drawing shows Charles Dickens, his wife, Kate, and her sister in 1843, the year after his triumphal American tour. At 31 he was already a famous writer.

offence against the laws of decorum that I felt in common with many others the blood tingling in my cheeks.

And yet, despite the moral indignation, the sour-grape grumblings, the sharp business practices, and the mass hysteria of the assembled social lions of America, determined to honor Dickens with might and "mane," the Boz Ball was acknowledged by the majority of Americans the most recherché event of the decade and remembered for many years. In Philip Hone's words, it was "the greatest affair in modern times . . . the fullest libation upon the altar of the muses." As for the minority, their sentiments were reflected in one of the comic songs written upon the arrival of Dickens in Boston, a song that was to prove clairvoyant in its prediction of what was in store for the author of *Pickwick* during his transatlantic visit:

for bankruptcy and that "several names appeared in both." In its later account of the ball itself, the editor commented dryly, "Boz maniacs are supremely ridiculous and justify all the jibes of the Halls and Trollopes. . . . We learn that the *patricians* sat in the boxes in half dress, to look on the *plebeians* who danced on the stage in full dress." The whole affair, the writer concluded, "has exhibited us thus far as a vain, mercurial, inconsiderate people, who cannot discriminate between cordial yet dignified hospitality and wild, headlong, senseless acclamation."

Even one of the fortunate "3,000" found himself distressed by the proceedings and wrote to a friend, the young American novelist Richard Henry Dana:

I intended to see Dickens at the ball in the evening. But he was besieged by such a regiment of militia officers and committeemen, the former so bedizened and bespangled with epaulettes and brass buttons and the latter displaying the insignia of rank in the shape of ribbons inserted wherever the button holes would permit to such an alarming extent that in the pusillanimity of my heart I remained in the background. This ball was got up by some of the small fry in the literary world. At the instance of some nincompoop he was received at his entrance into the ballroom with cheers and paraded around to the tune of God Save the Queen agreeably varied by Hail Columbia, Happy Land, and Yankee Doodle. The whole transaction was such an

They'll tope thee, Boz, they'll soap thee, Boz—
  Already they begin!
They'll dine thee, Boz, they'll wine thee, Boz,
  They'll stuff thee to the chin!
They'll smother thee with victuals, Boz,
  With fish, and flesh, and chickens;
Our authorlings will bore thee, Boz,
  And hail thee, "Cousin Dickens."
While ladies—'spite thy better half—
  Blue, yellow, foul, and fair,
Wilt coax thee for thy autograph,
  And likewise locks of hair!

Beware, Boz! Take care, Boz!
  Of forming false conclusions,
Because a certain sort of folk
  Do mete thee such oblations;
For these are not the people, Boz,
  These templars of the cork,
No more than a church steeple, Boz,
  Is Boston or New York.

Ada Nisbet, an associate professor of English at UCLA, has written several studies of nineteenth-century Anglo-American relations and is now planning a book on Dickens and America.

Fire-Eating Farmer
of the Confederacy

CONTINUED FROM PAGE 25

Virginia, even though he charged five dollars a year. His was the coaxing, explaining, and counseling voice. He wrote nearly half of each 64-page issue and took up every subject of interest to farmers. He proved a reliable debunker of farming myths and inundated his readers with the latest information from agricultural scientists in this country and abroad. He weeded out all references to politics as outside the pale. Carried away by the response to his efforts, he learned "I can with pleasure write rapidly for twelve or more hours in the day or night and until it is necessary to rest my cramped right hand."

It was not only about marl that he wrote, although the printing of his original essay, expanded into a book in 1832, brought on a great public interest in marl. He spread the gospel of crop rotation, proper plowing, the use of animal and vegetable manures, reclamation of swampland, proper drainage systems, and the economic use of slave labor. Almost all of what he offered came from personal experience and had the ring of authority. But, because he earnestly believed that farming was an entirely serious business, there was not a spark of humor in anything he wrote.

A new era in farming was beginning to arise under his guidance, and Ruffin might have spent his lifetime as an editor. But when banking reforms grew into a national issue after the Panic of 1837, he could not control his hot temper. As far as he was concerned, bankers were natural enemies of farmers. Short statements began cropping up in the *Farmers' Register* about the banking class, which he vilified as a storehouse of "lying, fraud and swindling." When some readers protested this outpouring, he launched a separate magazine, the *Bank Reformer,* in 1841. Here he hammered away at the prevalent banking system as a "paper-money system . . . to enable those who have earned or accumulated nothing by labor to exchange this *nothing* for the *something* and often the *everything* earned by the labor of others."

With this new publishing enterprise, Ruffin ran headlong into the encrusted political leadership of Virginia. They found his views dangerous and moved to destroy him. First a dribble and then an avalanche of subscription cancellations came to the *Farmers' Register* office. The loss of revenue forced Ruffin to abandon both publications.

Ruffin was bitter and angry now. All his work, he felt, had been for naught. He had to be the complete leader to all farmers or nothing at all. When the Virginia State Board of Agriculture, which he had helped organize and on which he served as first corresponding secretary, seemed unappreciative of his status, he resigned in a huff.

In 1842, hurt by the stigma now attached to his name, he leaped at the opportunity offered him by Governor James H. Hammond of South Carolina to serve as that state's agricultural surveyor. For a year he busied himself roaming South Carolina to locate marl beds, analyze soil, and discuss scientific farming. He thought little of his work there, but Hammond later hailed him as "one of the few benefactors of mankind whose services have been appreciated by the world, while still living." Ruffin, however, remained unconvinced, although reports from the Palmetto State after his departure revealed an exciting spurt of interest in scientific farming, guided strongly by the summary of the year's work, his *Report of the Commencement and Progress of the Agricultural Survey of South Carolina,* a landmark in the state's agricultural history.

His success in South Carolina did little to ease his hurt feelings upon his return to Virginia. Rather than remain among his old planter acquaintances, he moved northward to a new estate on the Pamunkey River in Hanover County. His face creased into a sneer when his neighbors, before his departure, presented him with silverware and drank to the toast: "Edmund Ruffin, the pioneer of marling, the author of *An Essay on Calcareous Manures* and editor of the *Farmers' Register*—Imperishable works of genius and industry."

Appropriately enough, he called his new estate Marlbourne. It was a horribly run-down plantation, but it was what he wanted in order to hide from public view. It was also his grand opportunity to put all his theories to work. First he got rid of his white supervisor and raised Jem Sykes, a slave, to the post of first assistant. Next, instead of using plain marl, he spread almost 300,000 bushels of "greensand" onto his land during the next five years. The greensand contained potash and phosphoric acid, in addition to marl. He installed covered drains, carefully rotated his crops, and used the newfangled McCormick reapers and threshing machines. Soon visitors were crowding his land and watching with awe as he ran the trim farm on a clockwork basis. From a first-year loss, his profits rose to more than 20 per cent of his investment in his fifth year.

After his spectacular success at Marlbourne he returned once more to his former life of speaking and writing. In 1845 a new Virginia State Agricultural Society was established and Ruffin was named president. He declined this honor because he was too close to his publishing debacle. However, in 1852, when the society honored him with the toast, "Not Edmund Ruffin of Prince George, of Petersburg, of Hanover, but Edmund Ruffin of Virginia," he finally accepted the presidency. The encomium was belated, but nevertheless appreciated.

By 1850 his standing as the South's farmer supreme was beyond challenge. Early in that decade the governor of Virginia in his annual message pointed out that, chiefly owing to marling, the value of land in the Tidewater district had risen by more than seventeen million dollars between 1838 and 1850. Although he did not mention Ruffin by name, it was obvious to his listeners that Ruffin was being honored.

Ruffin was sixty in 1854. He had fought the good fight and had emerged as one of his state's leading citizens. He agreed to serve as agricultural commissioner of Virginia that year, although he said it would not be for long. He was still writing articles on farming, but he hoped to taper off on that work, too. He pushed avidly for the establishment of agricultural colleges as state-supported institutions as if this were to be his crowning effort; then in 1855 he published a nostalgic collection of his fourteen best essays on agriculture. All indications were that he would soon retire.

He would have, too, had not the slavery issue embroiled the nation. The man who had helped save the institution of slavery could not let it disappear now under the blast of Abolitionist threats. Sickly and tired as he was, he determined to save the South a second time.

The sense of power from his farming success goaded him on to take a strong lead in the secession fight. With new inspiration, his vigor expanded; he became rabid on the subjects of slavery and secession. With an exultant smile in his eyes, he could prove from esoteric Biblical sources the sanctified nature of slavery. When these were exhausted he could proceed to endless economic and sociological arguments. It was the northern factory worker who was really a slave, he pointed out. He wrote frenziedly for various newspapers and magazines, revealing a vile hatred of northerners. Even Webster's dictionary was the "embodiment of the Yankee language and authority for Yankee deviation from Standard English."

The Kansas-Nebraska fight enraged Ruffin further, and after the election of Buchanan in 1856 he set his mind unswervingly on secession. Friendly railroad proprietors had begun slipping the old farmer free passes so that he could traverse the South in a call for secession. The lack of interest in some places appalled him. He wrote a series of four pungent articles which appeared in the popular *DeBow's Review* on "Consequences of Abolition Agitation," criticizing the South for lagging in its duty. To put an end to southern hesitation, Ruffin and the rabble-rousing William L. Yancey of Alabama organized the League of United Southerners in 1858. Yet, though several local clubs came into being, Ruffin could find no sustained interest in secession. Not until late in 1859 did he find cause for rejoicing. The occasion was John Brown's raid at Harpers Ferry. He scribbled in his diary that it was a godsend "to stir the sluggish blood of the South." Believing firmly that the Abolitionists would attempt to save Brown, he hurried to Harpers Ferry and then to Charles Town, Virginia (now West Virginia), to be at the center of this momentous event. If Brown were rescued before his execution, Ruffin argued, it "would be the immediate cause of separation of Southern and Northern states."

He walked the streets of Charles Town before the date of execution, talking secession to every group he could buttonhole. He was like a drunk on a binge. He made some converts, but not enough to suit him. With a firm hand he gripped one of John Brown's pikes and promenaded the streets holding it aloft and displaying a label he had attached to it: "Sample of the favors designed for us by our Northern Brethren." Acquiring a larger supply of pikes, he sent one to each southern governor.

When the day of execution arrived on December 2 and no attempt to rescue Brown was forthcoming, Ruffin talked his way into a cadet corps in order to have a front row view of the hanging. In great and hungry detail, he wrote of the execution in his diary. For a moment, at least, he had found a northerner as fanatical as himself and he gushed about Brown's "insensibility to danger and death."

In 1860 he quickened his pace. He helped organize ladies' shooting clubs as a civilian defense measure. To attract attention, he wore homespun of a poor quality, and on his hat a cockade. *Leslie's* magazine hooted at him: "The old man goes about from Convention to Convention, a political Peter the Hermit preaching secession wherever he goes." That year he wrote his last book, *Anticipations of the Future*. The work was a prophecy of events between 1864 and 1870. In it he had Lincoln serving one term and Seward succeeding him. He forecast that Lincoln would refrain from bullying the South, to prevent secession. But secession would come, said

Ruffin, under Seward. In the imaginary war that followed, the North grew steadily weaker; the South stronger.

The year 1861 saw the culmination of all his dreams. Not only did he witness the outbreak of fighting between the South and North, but he also played a personal role in major events.

South Carolina had boldly seceded from the Union in December of 1860. When Ruffin heard that hotheads there planned to attack Union-held Fort Sumter in Charleston Harbor unless it surrendered, he packed a cheese, some crackers, and extra clothes and hurried to Charleston. To anyone who would listen, he told of his disgust with his native Virginia for not seceding.

On April 9 at the Charleston wharf, a gaunt little Ruffin boarded a boat for Morris Island past Fort Sumter. He had heard that the Iron Battery there was to attack if Major Robert Anderson were foolish enough to try to hold Sumter for the Yankees. When Ruffin reached Morris Island, great cheering arose, and he was invited to join the Palmetto Guards. He was also promised the first shot of the coming war.

Ruffin described this momentous event of April 12 in his diary:

"By order of Gen. Beauregard, made known the afternoon of the 11th, the attack was to be commenced by the first shot at the fort being fired by the Palmetto Guards and from the Iron Battery. In accepting and acting upon this highly appreciated compliment, that company had made me its instrument. . . .

"Before 4 A.M. the drums beat for parade, and our company was speedily on the march which they were to man. At 4:30 a *signal* shell was thrown from a mortar battery at Fort Johnson, which had been before ordered to be taken as the command for immediate attack. . . . The night before, when expecting to attack, Captain Cuthbert had notified me that his company requested of me to discharge the first cannon to be fired. . . . Of course I was highly gratified by the compliment, and delighted to perform the service—which I did. The shell struck the Fort at the northeast angle of the parapet."

Loud hurrahs went up for Ruffin. The South ecstatically hailed the old man, who had become a patriotic symbol, while the New York *Post* stormed: "A piece of the first hemp . . . stretched in South Carolina should be kept for venerable and blood-thirsty *Ruffian*." Affectionately treated as the man of the hour wherever he traveled in the South, Ruffin affected a studied trick of halting upon being recognized by cheering crowds and bowing his head slowly and aloofly in acknowledgment. The claim by a Beauregard aide that the first shot of the war was actually the supposed signal shot from Fort Johnson, fired by Captain George S. James, and not the Morris Island blast by Ruffin, did nothing to dim Ruffin's new reputation.

When the First Battle of Manassas loomed in the summer of 1861, Ruffin determined to see action there, too. He found the Palmetto Guards at Fairfax Courthouse, not far from Washington, and for old times sake they let him join up again as a "temporary" private. Old and bent now, he dug trenches and tried to keep up with the younger men in their marches. The biscuits they chewed were too hard for his teeth, and since his tent was open at both ends the rain drenched him thoroughly. Secretly he hoped that he would be killed in battle, for he thought this would be a fitting end to his career. If not, he hoped that he would prove a hero.

And a hero of sorts he became, too. When the Union troops retreated toward Centreville, Ruffin was among the Rebels along their route. In a sense, as important as the shot he fired at Fort Sumter was another that he made on the Suspension Bridge over Cub Run. In the words of his compatriots, it was this shot that turned the Yankee retreat into a stampede.

Excitedly, Ruffin wrote in his diary:

"Our advance guard gave the information of the enemy being ahead and near to our front. Our front, to which Kemper's artillery had previously been charged, was at the crest of a long hill, down the gentle and uniform descent of which the turnpike road extended in a perfectly straight course to the Suspension Bridge over Cub Run. . . . The line of our march in pursuit, along the turnpike road, had been the same track of one large body of the routed fleeing Yankees. These had reached the bridge over Cub Run, and there filled the road with a closely packed crowd of soldiers, artillery trains, baggage wagons, ambulances, etc.

"The first wagon had just been driven upon the bridge to pass over when the first gun (my gun) was fired from Kemper's battery. . . . Some of the shot from this first discharge struck one or more of the horses of the foremost wagon. In their pain and fright they suddenly turned, upset the wagon so as to barricade the whole width of the bridge and effectively foreclosed any other wheel-carriages or horse from moving on. The whole mess of fugitives immediately got out of the track, and all escaped who could, on foot as quickly as possible. . . . Thus all the wagons and artillery were abandoned and everything else left by the terrified fugitives."

The joy of the Manassas victory made Ruffin positive that the North would soon give up. But the cost of his own service in that battle ran high. He was deaf now from the artillery noise, and a nervous condition made reading or writing difficult. He was to suffer further pain when the Yankees did not ask for peace.

The war took on a grimness that he did not expect. It was to be a fight to the finish. He took to meeting troops at Richmond and other places in order to cheer them. His appearance stirred up excitement, but he no longer had a boastful twinkle in his eye. During the Peninsula Campaign of 1862, it was rumored that the North considered him an important prize of war. After the Yankees left, he visited his old home at Coggin's Point and found it almost completely destroyed, with a mocking scrawl on a battered wall: "This house belonged to a Ruffinly son-of-a-bitch."

The Second Battle of Manassas in August, 1862, revived his optimism. However, when news of Gettysburg came to him the following year, his belief in an ultimate victory for the South vanished. But he would not have her surrender. His mouth set grimly, he gave all but a pittance of his money to the Confederate treasury. In May, 1864, he suffered a crushing blow when he heard that Union forces had occupied his precious Marlbourne and destroyed his library.

The end was not far off. In April, 1865, he wrote in his diary: "Richmond was evacuated last night. All Virginia, and this eastern part certainly and speedily, will be occupied or over-run by the vindictive and atrocious enemy. . . ." Of his eleven children, only three were alive. A favorite son, Julian, had died in the battle of Drewry's Bluff. His grief over Julian was great, even though he wrote in his diary that he had become devoid of all emotions. His entire life, he felt, had been for naught—marling and seceding, a strange combination.

The demise of the Confederacy with Lee's surrender was too much for Ruffin. On June 18, 1865, he pulled out his diary for the last time. He was penniless, sick, hungry; his slaves had deserted him; his land was ruined. Badly palsied, he nevertheless wrote in a bold hand: "And now, with my latest writing and utterance, and with what will be near my latest breath, I hereby repeat and would willingly proclaim my unmitigated hatred to Yankee rule—to all political, social and business connections with Yankees, and the perfidious, malignant and vile Yankee race."

Laying down his pen, Ruffin picked up a pistol and shot himself. Like the Virginia fields he had raised to fertility and then had helped destroy by the gun, Ruffin's life had completed its circle.

Alfred Steinberg is a free-lance writer of history and reporter of the Washington scene. He collaborated with Senator Tom Connally on his autobiography and is currently writing a biography of Eleanor Roosevelt.

Apostle to the Indians CONTINUED FROM PAGE 9

When Eliot began his Bible translation there was no assurance it would ever be printed, yet he continued at it through the years, trusting in Providence and in the London society. He did not trust in vain, for—as that unpractical man shrewdly realized—such a project was attuned to the very premises on which the society was founded. Its governors agreed to underwrite the expenses of the Indian Bible.

The *Up-Biblum* was printed by Samuel Green at the Cambridge Press, housed in the Indian College inside the Harvard Yard. Directly and indirectly this undertaking was worth the then very large sum of £1,000 a year to the Boston commercial community.

Eliot completed his translation in 1659. That same year printing was begun, and almost at once the society shipped an additional press to Cambridge. Special type had to be sent as well, the Indian language requiring a double *o* logotype and more than the normal proportions of *o*'s, *k*'s, and *q*'s.

The final chapters of Revelation were printed in 1663. Fifteen hundred copies of the *Up-Biblum* were run off, 200 copies being bound in stout leather for the immediate use of the Indians. This was the first Bible printed in America, the earliest example in history of the translation and printing of the entire Bible as a means of evangelization. It was Eliot's most durable monument.

King Charles' acceptance of the sudden and politic dedication of the *Up-Biblum* was gracious, considering the fact that only three years before Eliot, in a slim volume called *The Christian Commonwealth*, had applauded Cromwell, denounced Charles I as anti-Christ, and anathematized the Lords and Commons.

The following dozen years were to climax Eliot's labors. Captain Daniel Gookin, a layman of some military and political prominence in the colony, was appointed superintendent of the Praying Indians and became Eliot's principal colleague. The original settlement at Natick throve mightily, and additional towns were set up at Stoughton, Grafton, Marlboro, Littleton, and Tewksbury. Eliot composed an Indian Primer, an Indian Grammar, and an Indian Psalter and made a translation of Baxter's *Call to the Unconverted*. In 1674 there were two established Indian

churches, fourteen Indian towns, and 1,100 Praying Indians.

An unusual glimpse of Eliot comes to us from a novel source. In the mid-seventeenth century the Jesuit Father Druillette was sent by the governor of Canada to Boston to discuss commercial relations. Although Jesuits were nominally under sentence of death in Massachusetts, Father Druillette was received cordially both by Governor Endicott and by Governor Bradford of Plymouth. On one of his journeys he was an overnight guest of Eliot. That meeting of the priest and the Puritan conversing by the fireside as best they could in church and school Latin became the subject of a number of sentimental Victorian illustrations.

Eliot's vision of a Christianized Indian fellowship of thriving and expanding towns was shattered in 1675 by the outbreak of King Philip's War. Philip was the son of Massasoit, the sachem of the Rhode Island Wampanoags, whose early treaty with Plymouth banned any missionaries within his territory. More instinctively hostile to the whites than his politic father, Philip carried this anti-Christian bias even further. Once on a chance meeting with Eliot he had twisted a button of the latter's coat, telling him he cared no more for the Gospel than he did for that button.

To Philip's innate hostility was added his resentment at the encroaching whites. The old Pawtucket chieftain Passaconaway had warned him that though he might harm the colonists, they would in the end surely destroy him. That might be true, Philip thought, but only if he failed to strike in time. He planned with much cunning for a federation of tribes from Long Island Sound to the Penobscot that would rise at a given signal and exterminate the English settlements. For four years he made his preparations, formed secret alliances with the other tribes, collected guns and munitions and supplies, and planned his strategy.

The outbreak, in the middle of June, was sudden, bloody, and disastrous for the colonists. From Springfield east a hundred miles to within sight of Boston the towns went up in flames, and women and children were butchered with malignant savagery. Although Waban had warned the colonists some time before, they were unprepared. Before the militia could muster any effective counterattack the western garrisons were besieged and in some cases annihilated. No small town or isolated farm was safe. Terror of the savages reinforced all the colonists' earlier prejudices. Praying or not, an Indian was an Indian, better locked up, best dead.

Eliot's Indians lived in danger of their lives. Sometimes they were murdered out of hand, as at Chelmsford, or, as at Marlboro, seized and marched to the Boston jail. Yet in spite of ill will, suspicion, and harsh treatment which was to grow harsher, the great majority of the Praying Indians remained loyal. There were exceptions. James the Printer, who had helped print Eliot's *Up-Biblum*, abandoned his press and his hand-me-downs to put on war paint with Philip, as did Old Jethro, an Indian preacher Eliot had trained, who was later taken prisoner and hanged.

Eliot and Gookin did all they could to protect the lives and substance of their wards; but they were increasingly isolated by the hysterical clamor against the Praying Indians. Gookin's life was threatened in the streets of Boston. When Eliot's boat tipped over in the harbor and was nearly run down by another boat, several people said it was a pity he had not drowned.

At the autumn period of Philip's greatest successes, the colonists packed off the Praying Indians from Natick and the other towns just before the harvest and shipped them down Boston Harbor to Deer Island. There they were left, women and children and old men indifferently, to shift for themselves on that bleak drumlin lying open to the Atlantic. Eliot went to the water front to see the miserable converts embark, his most faithful among them—his ministers, his teachers, his interpreters. Whenever he could he visited them that winter, bringing small amounts of corn, provisions, and odds and ends of clothes. Those who survived did so for the most part by grubbing for clams and shellfish, threatened even there by some of the more hotheaded colonists, who as a reprisal for burnt villages were for going to Deer Island to kill the lot.

Yet through all their wretchedness the Indians still remained firm in their affection for Eliot. And when some of the less fanatical and more practical-minded colonists decided to try to raise an Indian scouting company from among them, sixty volunteered. In the end, Indian aid to the English was substantial. The Praying Indians, resuming their forest ways, killed over 400 of the enemy, and Gookin maintained that they "turned ye balance to ye English side, so that ye enemy went down ye wind amain."

The war lasted until the middle of the following year. Philip was finally surrounded and brought to bay in Mount Hope Swamp in Rhode Island, a Praying Indian firing the shot that finished him. The militiamen found him lying in the mud, "a doleful, great, naked, dirty beast." They cut off his head and brought it to Plymouth, where it stood impaled for the next quarter of a century.

With the end of this threat the Praying Indians were allowed to leave Deer Island for their old homes, but only a poor minority survived. Whatever creative spark Eliot had managed to kindle in them had gone out. The end of Philip was the knell of the Massachusetts Indians. Over Eliot's distressed protests the war captives, including Philip's wife and young children, were sold into slavery in the West Indies. Where fourteen thriving Indian towns had existed, there were now only four listless and dwindling settlements.

The London society, however, continued its help. Most of the Indian Bibles had been burnt or destroyed during the war, and Eliot prepared a revised edition with the help of his friend John Cotton of Plymouth, who knew the language even better than he did. He still visited his remaining Indians when he could, although less frequently now that old age was on him.

John Eliot was to live another fifteen years, a patriarchal figure, revered now in the harmlessness of his broken dream, one of the last thin links with that first generation from across the ocean. His Praying Indians were no longer a problem in the expanding colony, and the bitterness was glossed over now. From Roxbury to Boston he had become such a time-accustomed figure over half a century that he seemed almost beyond time, and a saying grew up that Massachusetts could not come to an end as long as the Reverend John Eliot lived.

He himself knew that his time was almost out and how vain most of it had been. "There is a cloud," he wrote finally, "a dark cloud upon the work of the Gospel among the poor Indians."

He lived to see his wife Anne and four of his six children with Christ, his Cromwell with Christ, Charles with the Devil, God's Commonwealth pilloried, and every hand against his copper-colored children. And he remembered his *Up-Biblum*. Cotton Mather, pursuing a fancy of which he was fond, discovered that the anagram of his name was Toile.

John Eliot waited for the end with desire. For him the Great Perhaps was a certainty. When he was very old he liked to say that John Cotton and Richard Mather and the friends of his youth would suspect him of having gone the wrong way because he remained so long behind them. At the last, when he was dying, he dismissed the young clergymen who had come to pray superfluously over him. "Welcome Joy!" were his last words.

Francis Russell became interested in John Eliot while a student at Roxbury Latin School, America's oldest private school, which Eliot founded in 1645. Now a resident of Wellesley Hills, Massachusetts, Mr. Russell contributed "Lost Elegance" to the June, 1957, issue of AMERICAN HERITAGE.

Bonnet, Book, and Hatchet CONTINUED FROM PAGE 55

while Mrs. Nation and Mrs. White were chopping away at the glossy-smooth bar, raising chips of a size and depth beyond the ability of most women. Tucker knew instantly who his callers were. He grabbed the house revolver from behind the bar and advanced with the idea he would frighten these vixens. Frighten? Mrs. Nation met him halfway, lunged, and swung her weapon viciously at his head. Tucker dodged, snatched the hatchet from her hand, fired two shots into the rococo ceiling, then went through the rear door at a dead run, shouting for the police.

Carry Nation gave a bellow of triumph. From one of her companions she took another hatchet and attacked the big mirror. While glass was still falling, she swept her weapon, much like a stick on a picket fence, along the long row of glassware on the back bar, and shouted her special kind of abuse at the absent bartender. "How do you do," she called, "you maker of drunkards and widows?"

While the acolytes, Mrs. White and Miss Southard, continued to perform as well as their limited imaginations permitted, Mrs. Nation went ahead with feverish experimentation. "The arm of God smiteth!" she cried and grabbed the cash register from its moorings on the bar. With little more than a genteel grunt she lifted the heavy machine above her head, then heaved it halfway across the saloon, to watch it crash to the floor, with its bell ringing No Sale as never before, while tiny wheels and bolts and silver rolled in happy confusion. It had been a mighty effort. She had been granted the strength of giants.

Mrs. Nation paused only to badger the still-absent bartender again. "Good morning," she shouted, "you destroyer of men's souls!" then turned her attention into demolition channels. First she strode up to face the monstrous refrigerator. With the hammer end of her hatchet she smashed the lock, opened the vast door, which she grasped firmly in her two hands, and tore it fair from its hinges. Taking up her hatchet again, she cut the rubber tube which conducted the beer from the tanks to the faucets, and then, using the tube as a hose, sprayed good St. Louis beer over the walls and ceilings, to cascade down and drench herself and co-workers in malted foam. A squad of police entered to arrest the crusaders, after disarming them.

The whole gorgeous story went out over the wires, and Carry and Hatchet went into the folklore of the nation. Cartoonists got busy. Almost before one knew it, too, miniature hatchets labeled with her name were being hawked in cities from coast to coast and offered for sale by news butchers on trains.

Other hatchet women appeared as if by magic. In Danville, Kansas, a tall, lean female named Mary Sheriff wrecked a local joint with a hatchet, collected a group of women she called the Flying Squadron of Jesus, and swept through Harper County like a plague, attacked sample rooms in Attica, Anthony, and other towns and leaving them in dreadful condition; while in Elk County there arose a smasher fit to talk with Mrs. Nation herself. She was Mrs. McHenry. In a brief war she laid waste to every joint in the county, then moved on to new successes all over the state. Other imitators erupted, if only briefly, in Illinois, Indiana, and Ohio. These plagiarists had no effect on Mrs. Nation's fame save to enhance it.

In that day a character of the celebrity of Carry Nation was headed surely for the lyceum circuit. Billed variously, according to neighborhood, as The Home Defender, The Smasher, The Wrecker of Saloons, The Woman with the Hatchet, she toured much of the United States. She began publication of a weekly paper, *The Hatchet*. She went to Washington for the express purpose of talking to—not with—President Theodore Roosevelt, to warn him of the hideous example his daughter Alice was setting for pure womanhood by smoking cigarettes.

The White House guard was polite but firm; he met Mrs. Nation before she got to the door to inform her it was not possible to see the President. When she began a harangue about cigarette fiends, the guard broke in.

"Madam," he said, "do not make a lecture here."

Mrs. Nation sighed and left with a well-turned phrase: "I suppose you have the same motto here in the White House that they have in the saloons, 'All the Nations Welcome Except Carry.'" She went away to tell a newspaper reporter that Roosevelt's predecessor, President McKinley, might have recovered from the wounds of his assassin "had not his blood been poisoned by nicotine," and left such dark inference as the reporter cared to form in regard to what might well happen to the Roosevelts.

Though a few individual members of the W.C.T.U. considered Carry Nation a true hero-martyr in the John Brown tradition, she was treated coolly, then with increasing hostility by virtually all of the Union. The excitement she created gradually died in the United States. She went abroad to lecture in the British Isles, where she appeared in the music halls and was greeted by large audiences and often with showers of eggs and vegetables. Finding on return that she was

120

in great danger of being wholly forgotten, she attacked the barroom in Washington's Union Depot, late in 1909, and wrought fearful havoc with *three* hatchets she told the police were Faith, Hope, and Charity. In the following January she made her last attack. It was, properly enough, in Butte, Montana, then, as now, a lively town, and it was directed at May Maloy's Dance Hall & Café. For the sake of the record, it was on January 26, 1910, when Carry Nation entered Miss Maloy's place with the avowed intention to destroy a painting, and was met at the entrance by the proprietor herself, a young and powerful woman, who went hammer-and-tongs at the astonished crusader. The encounter was brief, terrible, and one-sided. The old champ went down, and went away to Arkansas. On January 13, 1911, she was stricken while speaking against joints and jointists at Eureka Springs and died on June 9 in Evergreen Hospital, Leavenworth, Kansas.

In Mrs. Nation's day almost nobody had a good word for saloons. The brewers and distillers were inclined to let the saloonkeeper fight his own battles, smugly confident that more genteel vendors of their wares would take his place. Though the Anti-Saloon League ignored Carry Nation, her furious onslaught focused publicity on the liquor outlets, and she also forced Kansas and other pseudo-dry states—as one commentator put it—to "live up to their pretensions." He thought that "a whole host of temperance workers were unequal to her influence."

Carry Nation was a unique character in many ways, including the fact that she is best remembered by the symbol she made her own, much as an earlier American female, Miss Lizzie Borden of Fall River, Massachusetts, is remembered for a slightly larger symbol, which was the ax.

Vermont-born Stewart H. Holbrook lives in Portland, Oregon. He wrote his piece on Carry Nation for his diverting new book on reformers, Dreamers of the American Dream, *which, like his earlier classic,* The Age of the Moguls, *was written for Doubleday's "Mainstream of America" series.*

Great Man Eloquent CONTINUED FROM PAGE 79

Then old Henry Clay, already mortally ill, summoned the last of his strength to devise the nine measures known as the Compromise of 1850 and, dying on his feet, prevented the death of his country. His success was not immediate. Since it was a genuine compromise, it was furiously attacked by both Calhoun and Seward, and its fate wavered in the balance week after week and month after month. So evenly matched were the contestants that eventually it became plain that all depended upon Webster, who had so far said nothing.

On March 7 at last he rose to speak, ". . . not as a Massachusetts man, nor as a Northern man, but as an American . . . I speak today for the preservation of the Union. 'Hear me for my cause.'" They heard. They heeded. The squabbling continued for months, but eventually the compromise was adopted and the Civil War was postponed for ten years.

But Webster's reward was such denunciation from his own people as few American statesmen have had to endure. John Greenleaf Whittier, that singularly bloodthirsty Quaker, promptly consigned him to the tomb without waiting for an attending physician's certificate:

from those great eyes
The soul has fled:
When faith is lost, when honor dies,
The man is dead!

and less melodious calumniators poured cruder vituperation on him wherever two or three lunatics were gathered together.

Yet every measurement known to statistics shows clearly that from 1820 on the South had been steadily losing and the North steadily gaining in relative strength. Nevertheless, when war did break in 1861, it took every ounce of Northern strength to win through four years of the bloodiest fighting in modern times. Few Americans stop to realize that, in proportion to the numbers engaged, the American Civil War was several times as deadly as either World War I or World War II. If it had come ten years earlier the border states would almost certainly have gone with the South, and the outcome can hardly be doubted.

Henry Clay's Compromise of 1850 saved this Union; and Daniel Webster saved the compromise.

But it was not by logic that he did it. Logically, he was a Massachusetts man, a Northern man, but emotionally he was an American; and the emotional appeal, not the logic, carried the compromise. More than that, it carried Daniel Webster into the hearts of an emotional people, and there he abides. We do not believe, we cannot believe, that knowledge, logic, might, or the Devil himself can prevail against a man who loves anything strongly enough to invite ruin in its defense.

This characteristic of human nature is the great

Webster enjoyed a country squire's life at Marshfield, his home near Plymouth, Mass., and there he died in October, 1852. "He had started small and poor," a friend said, "had risen great and high, and honorably had fought his way alone."

weakness of democracy, as has been vociferously proclaimed by every logician from Plato down. Alcibiades played upon it; so did Huey Long and Joe McCarthy and all the demagogues between. But under favorable circumstances it is also the great strength of democracy, as Webster, Lincoln, and the second Roosevelt instinctively recognized. It is the factor that transforms government from a science into an art, maddening the scientists, including—perhaps one should say especially—the social scientists, and inspiring poets and other irresponsible characters.

The obvious fact that democracy is—apparently incurably—emotional rather than logical is the despair of men who have subjected their minds to rigorous intellectual discipline, and who are therefore convinced that intellectual discipline is the only conceivable approach to truth. Thus when they perceive that the great heroes of democracy seem to bear more family likeness to Roscius, the actor, than to Aristotle, the philosopher, they tend to despair of democracy. Webster is a case in point. He was certainly a great constitutional lawyer, which is to say, a logician; but he became immortal only when he abandoned his logic and appealed to the emotions as frankly as Cleon of Athens ever did. The legal precedents he set—as, for example, his arguments for the bank, for and then against free trade, and on municipal and international law—have been largely superseded or abandoned, but the moods he established have endured for more than a hundred years. Superficially, this suggests that demagoguery casts its works in bronze, while statecraft carves in butter, which is a patent absurdity.

What the rigid logicians tend to overlook is that emotionalism as a political instrument is not monolithic. It is divided into separate and antipodal branches, one of which relies on love, the other on hate as its chief agency. Hope is subsidiary to love as fear is to hate. The artists, as distinguished from the

scientists, in government can be classified accordingly. If one relies on the emotions of hate and fear of the enemy, it is safe to classify him with Alcibiades; but if he relies on love of country and hope for the future, there you have Pericles.

There is not the slightest doubt on which side of the line Daniel Webster's appeal to the emotions lay. He spoke as an American. He spoke for the future. He was extravagant, yes; he was turgid and bombastic, if you will. But his worst extravagance and bombast were never designed to foment hatred and fear, but always to stimulate love and pride. Therefore the people, greatly needing both, have looked with an indulgent eye on his faults and frailties and, because he spurred them in the direction of greatness, deemed him, and still deem him, a great man.

True, the eye with which they have regarded him is not only indulgent, but a little sardonic. When his last words were reported, folklore quickly invented an explanation of the utterance. People said that the physician remarked to an attendant when the end was obviously at hand, "If he is still living in an hour, give him brandy," whereupon Daniel Webster with his dying breath murmured, "I still live."

Never mind. Whom the American people love, they laugh at. It has always been so, and it will be so until the character of the nation is changed. If his spirit could return to observe what has come of the nation that he saved, it is easy to believe that it would be less impressed by the miraculous changes that have taken place than by the lack of any change in the common people's love of and pride in their country. And seeing this lack of change the disembodied spirit could repeat, "I still live."

The latest of Gerald W. Johnson's many books on politics and the American social scene is The Square Pegs. *He wrote "Dynamic Victoria Woodhull" for the June, 1956, issue of* AMERICAN HERITAGE.

"The Gray-Eyed Man of Destiny"

CONTINUED FROM PAGE 29

force, which, though ten times as large, had consumed so much brandy to rouse their courage before the battle that the Americans won an easy victory. Walker now decided on the one really brilliant stroke of generalship in his career. The entire Legitimist army was at Rivas, leaving Granada, the government seat, undefended. Walker loaded his entire force, now increased to 350 by recruits from the United States and native volunteers, on the Transit Line's steamer, sailed them up Lake Nicaragua and advanced at night on the unsuspecting city. They surged over an unmanned barricade and rushed at the double into the main plaza, encountering only a few scattered shots from the skeleton garrison, who then turned and fled. In a matter of hours, with the loss of one soldier, Walker was master of the enemy capital.

By his capture of Granada, Walker put himself in a position which might very possibly have led in time to his dominance of all Central America and even, just possibly, to the eventual conquest of Cuba as well, and its consolidation into a Central American-Caribbean empire of sorts, which, based on slavery, would be a firm ally of the southern states. It was a stirring prospect and the chances are that Walker dimly glimpsed its glitter. His failings, however, were a stubborn refusal to heed the advice of experienced advisers and an overwhelming impatience, the occupational disease of almost all dictators. And these faults betrayed him.

For a while, however, he played his newly won trumps with considerable skill. First, he released about a hundred political prisoners rotting in chains and dungeons under Granada's great cathedral. The day after the capture of the city he attended Mass at the cathedral, accompanied by many of his officers, and soon won the powerful support of the clergy by his respect for church property and traditions. Two weeks later the Legitimist commander acknowledged defeat and came into Granada to arrange a peace. Walker put on a great show for his entry by lining the streets and the plaza with his heavily armed followers and also armed and paraded a large number of male travelers stranded in the city because of the closure of the Transit route.

The result was a treaty which ended hostilities and named Patricio Rivas, an innocuous Legitimist, temporary president of the united republic. It appointed William Walker as commander in chief of the combined armies. The Legitimist garrison at Fort San Carlos and another farther down the San Juan River then abandoned their posts, and the Transit Line was again open to free movement. Landing with 58 men, William Walker had, in effect, captured Nicaragua in a little more than four months.

But only a few months later, in February, 1856, war broke out with Nicaragua's southern neighbor, the republic of Costa Rica, which raised an army of 9,000 men and declared war on Walker's "bandits." To compound his difficulties, Walker rashly decided to seize the steamers and properties of the Transit Company. Commodore Cornelius Vanderbilt had built up this line and had given, at first, every aid and assistance to Walker, who, he hoped, would bring peace and order to the revolution-wracked country. But Walker, whose knowledge of warfare in the financial jungle was limited, chose to line up with a faction seeking to oust Vanderbilt from control.

The old Commodore's wrath, when he heard of the confiscation, was said to have been terrible beyond description. He not only suspended the sailing of all Transit ships to Nicaragua, thus cutting Walker's supply line, but began intriguing both with the Costa Ricans and with Walker's puppet, President Rivas. Shortly after the Costa Rican army crossed the border, President Rivas went into revolt and appealed for help to the three little countries to the north—Guatemala, El Salvador, and Honduras. Walker met this crisis by assuming formal control of the government. On July 12, 1856, with a grand parade through the main square of Granada, he took the oath of office as president of Nicaragua. The American minister to Nicaragua, John H. Wheeler, a friend of Walker's, rashly took it upon himself to recognize the new government, but when the news reached Washington, Secretary of State Marcy recalled Wheeler and forced his resignation.

Some of Walker's proclamations, during the months between his formal accession to power and his downfall, were drastic. He confiscated many of the natives' estates to raise money, placed English on an equal legal basis with Spanish, and made changes in the land laws with the frank purpose of placing "a large portion of the land of the country in the hands of the white race"—meaning his own followers. Most potentially fateful was his decree relegalizing slavery, which had been abolished thirty years before. The significance of this decree was that Walker, rebuffed in his diplomatic overtures to the government at Washington, was casting his lot with the southern states in the impending Civil War. There is reason to believe that some of the southern leaders shared Walker's dream of a Latin American slave union as an ally in their own struggle.

None of these decrees ever went into effect because Walker's time was running out. By October he was under attack from the south by the Costa Ricans, and from the north by the combined armies of Guatemala, El Salvador, and Honduras. In this crisis Walker decided to evacuate Granada and to move his headquarters to the volcanic island of Ometepe on Lake Nicaragua. In order to deny his enemies the prestige of a conquest, he left his second in command, Charles Frederick Henningsen, a British soldier of fortune, at Granada with orders to destroy the city utterly.

Henningsen organized his men into demolition detachments and systematically began to blow up and burn the buildings section by section, while the hysterical natives streamed out of the city. Henningsen's men naturally found loot and wines and spirits in most of the houses they entered. Henningsen was unable to restrain his officers and they, in turn, lost all control of their men. As nightfall came, the city became an obscenity with flames shooting skyward, clouds of smoke hugging the roof tops, and groups of howling drunk, smoke-blackened filibusters screaming and reeling through the streets in an orgy of plunder and destruction. For two days and two nights this bedlam of annihilation rose to a crescendo as the crazed Americans drank and plundered, smashed and fired buildings, fell in a drunken stupor from which they would be awakened, likely as not, by the kicks of yelling and singing comrades, to rise dizzily and stagger on to smash and fire other buildings in the raging inferno of explosions and smoke—and to drink some more.

The enemy forces presently attacked the city from three different sides and one column seized the Guadalupe church, which stood on the street running between the wharf on Lake Nicaragua and the main plaza where Henningsen was rallying his men.

After setting fire to all the surrounding buildings, he began to fight his way, foot by foot, down the street toward the wharf. At first, many of the Americans were still half drunk, and some took to the bottle again in the face of such imminent danger. Somehow Henningsen finally got them sober and into a kind of order. A filibuster named Calvin O'Neal, whose brother had fallen in the first onslaughts, came to Henningsen in a frenzy of raging grief and asked permission to charge a body of 400 or 500 Guatemalan soldiers who could be seen forming in the distance. His commander gave him 32 picked Rifles. What followed was later described by Walker:

"O'Neal, barefooted and in his shirt sleeves, leaped on his horse, and calling on his Rifles to follow, dashed into the midst of the allies as they formed near the old church. The men, fired by the spirit of their leader, followed in the same fierce career, dealing death and destruction on the terrified foe. The allies were entirely unprepared for O'Neal's sudden, clashing charge, and they fell as heedless travellers before the blast of the simoom. The slaughter made by the thirty-two Rifles was fearful, and so far were O'Neal and his men carried by the 'rapture of the strife' that it was difficult for Henningsen to recall them to the Plaza. When they did return it was through streets almost blocked with the bodies of the Guatemalans they had slain."

By the next morning Henningsen had concentrated his forces in the main plaza and could count his strength. He had lost 23 men killed or captured and could muster only 227 soldiers fit for duty; he was burdened with 73 wounded and some 70 women and children and sick.

Two days later, on November 27, after blowing up a church on the plaza and destroying the nearby buildings (Henningsen was still carrying out his orders amidst the inferno), he poured a heavy artillery fire into the Guadalupe church and captured it by an immediately following assault by 60 picked Rifles. At once he moved all his forces and supplies into this large, strong building and prepared to withstand a siege until Walker could relieve him from the lake. His men had recovered from their debauchery and were willing to work and fight for their lives and for the protection of all the noncombatants. But the crowded and unsanitary conditions in the church, the food of mule and horse meat, the night chills and rains, and the stench from the unburied enemy dead outside brought much sickness to the 400 Americans huddled together, and cholera soon appeared as a far more dreadful foe than the enemy.

A ministering angel appeared amidst these terrible scenes, Mrs. Edward Bingham, the wife of an invalid actor who had brought his family to Nicaragua to take up one of Walker's grants of land to American settlers. From the time of her arrival she had nursed in the American hospitals, and in the Guadalupe church she constantly tended the sick and wounded with magnificent courage and complete self-sacrifice which gained her the deepest gratitude of all the soldiers. Finally, worn out and weak, she became another victim of the dreaded cholera and died within a few hours. Her children perished with her, but her invalid husband survived all the horrors of the siege and eventually reached California safely. Of all the Americans in Nicaragua this splendid woman showed the finest spirit.

For two harrowing weeks Henningsen held out

while Walker stood off Granada in the lake steamer *Virgen*, watching for a chance to extricate Henningsen's forces. Then, during the first week in December, 300 recruits arrived from New Orleans and San Francisco, well-equipped men in fine fettle and spoiling for a fight. Of these, 160 were organized as a relief force and placed under the command of the cavalry leader, Colonel John Waters. Waters landed his men and silently led them toward the city. By dawn he had stormed over all the enemy barricades and had joined Henningsen, with a loss of about a fourth of his men.

CULVER SERVICE

William Walker met his end in 1860 before a Honduran firing squad. Shortly before his death he had turned Catholic.

The Americans, who had been slowly extending their lines from the Guadalupe church down the street toward the water, quickly seized the wharf and embarked the survivors on the *Virgen* without enemy opposition.

General Henningsen, before he boarded the rescuing steamer, cast one last look back at the ruined city. Then he thrust a lance into the ground and to it attached a piece of rawhide upon which he had written, *Aqui fué Granada*—"Here was Granada."

Walker was not licked yet. He still commanded 900 men and controlled the Transit route, over which he expected several hundred reinforcements. But his enemies included, along with four sovereign states, the redoubtable Commodore Vanderbilt. Early in the autumn of 1856 the Commodore had dispatched to Costa Rica a young secret agent named Sylvanus Spencer with a well-planned scheme to seize the Transit route and bottle up the filibusters. With a small Costa Rican force and a boldness worthy of Walker himself, Spencer swooped down on one of Walker's garrisons, seized the river steamers, and cut off the filibuster reinforcements. By April, 1857, Walker's force was trapped at Rivas, with no hope of escape. By arrangement with the Central American armies he surrendered to an American naval officer, Commander Charles H. Davis, and was spirited off to New Orleans, where he received a hero's welcome.

Three more times William Walker and his followers attempted to invade Nicaragua without success. On the last attempt Walker surrendered to a British naval officer, who turned him over to the Honduran authorities, from whom he received short shrift. On September 12, 1860, he met his death before an adobe wall at the hands of a firing squad, an end which he had decreed so often for his political enemies. He was buried in an unmarked grave which Joaquin Miller commemorated in his poem "That Night in Nicaragua." Despite his ruthlessness and unappealing personality, Walker held the constant loyalty of many of his followers through all his later failures and, surprisingly enough, that of many of the natives as well. His men were beyond description daring. His able lieutenant, General Henningsen, years later wrote a fitting epitaph for these Homeric men of Nicaragua:

"I was on the Confederate side in many of the bloodiest battles of the late war; but I aver that if, at the end of that war, I had been allowed to pick five thousand of the bravest Confederate or Federal soldiers I ever saw, and could resurrect and pit against them one thousand of such men as lie beneath the orange trees of Nicaragua, I feel certain that the thousand would have scattered and utterly routed the five thousand within an hour. All military science failed, on a suddenly given field, before assailants who came on at run, to close with their revolvers, and who thought little of charging a battery, pistol in hand. . . .

"Such men do not turn up in the average of everyday life, nor do I ever expect to see their like again."

Edward S. Wallace is a historian and author of several books. His latest book, on which this article is based, is Destiny and Glory, *a history of the filibustering era. It is published by Coward-McCann.*

America: Curator of British Political Relics

CONTINUED FROM PAGE 15

cal extension of victory either by the executive or by the legislature would be the extinction of its rival as an equal branch of government; and, second, that many of the ordinarily political conflicts of the day, major and relatively trivial, become charged with constitutional significance, so that arguments of substance rapidly shift into arguments of constitutional and legal principle.

This is why conflicts between Crown and Parliament used to be so prolonged and bitter—compromise of a particular matter, perhaps not difficult on its merits, might by acting as a precedent tilt the whole balance of the system permanently to the Crown's disfavor. James I was perfectly correct, in his pedagogical way, in his listing of the royal prerogatives, but by writing them down and deducing a theoretical system of royal right from them he imperiled every privilege of Parliament. The same dilemma prevails under the American system, since although the Constitution helps to police the battle it does not avoid it. Thus, the President conducts foreign policy, while Congress has the right to declare war and to vote money; but foreign policy might lead to war. And

not only war but foreign policy itself, in these days of multi-billion-dollar foreign aid, requires money, and it may even, as the debate on the Eisenhower Doctrine illustrates, require a conditional declaration of war.

But it does not require matters of this moment to set senators off referring sententiously to "a grave constitutional issue" or savoring the oft-repeated tag, "This is a government of laws, not of men." Many times I have sat at the press table in a committee room of Congress listening to an apparently straightforward investigation only to find it veering off suddenly into a phase of the unending struggle between executive and legislature. It is then that I feel a new sense of reality breathed into English constitutional conflicts of an earlier age.

Keith Kyle is Washington correspondent of The Economist, *of London. He took his degree in history at Oxford, where he studied under A. J. P. Taylor. This article is taken from a talk he gave over the B.B.C. some months ago on "The Third Program," a kind of intelligent man's radio service which unfortunately has no U.S. counterpart.*

Farewell to Steam   TEXT CONTINUED FROM PAGE 61

trains today move no faster than at a sedate eighty miles an hour.)

Then, for a time, the railroad story becomes an extravagant tale of wild speculation, swindled bondholders, great systems devouring little ones, Wall Street coups, freight-rate scandals, rival financial titans. The harsh word is robber baron, and there are two notable quotations that come down to us from that era. There is the long argued-over retort of Vanderbilt, "The public be damned!" And there is the more characteristic remark, half aloud, half to himself, of another railroad king, on learning of a little railroad that no one had yet gobbled up: "Great Scott! Is there anything like that still left outdoors?" This was a time when, as Philip Guedalla noted, the names of railroad presidents were apt to be a good deal more significant than those of the occupants of the White House.

There was a railroad of song and folklore, where Jesse James stopped the mail car every night, where the cars just barely cleared the burning trestle, where the brave engineer kept his hand on the throttle,

where Dinah blew her horn all the day. But the most significant story is found in a series of railroad maps, by decades. Here at the start are only a few little wiggly lines around Charleston, Baltimore, New York, and Boston. Expanding steadily, as in an animated movie, they eventually envelop America in a giant spider web. They carry the emigrants west. They bring the crops east to be traded for the products of industry. They build cities, and woe betide those they pass by. They make the desert, as the orator said, bloom like a garden. They create wealth and opportunity. In 1848, old Number One of the Galena & Chicago Union smokes her way into Chicago, first steam locomotive to reach what would become the railroad capital of the country. The same story is told over and over again, of all the western cities, until the big balloon stacks appear under the southern California sky to touch off a boom that is not over yet. No wonder the railroad and the steam behemoth that moved along it were the symbols of America.

Steam could not last forever, any more than the stage coach, after the invention of a more efficient device. The perilous state of most railroad finances —beset by subsidized highway, air, and water competition, regulated as though a nineteenth-century monopoly still existed—required some drastic economies, and this the diesel provided. The public, deserting the railroad passenger services in droves, saw less and less of the changeover.

But steam is dying hard, nevertheless, and it retains an ever-growing army of admirers. They turn out by the thousands for one "last" ride after another; they swap endless pictures, spikes, tickets, old timetables, even recordings of railroad noises; and they jabber away happily in professional jargon. They organize a great many clubs and societies; they have authors and prophets like Lucius Beebe and Stewart Holbrook and Archie Robertson; they sustain several magazines of substantial circulation. They organize excursions, a sizable business, and even buy and maintain old engines. They attract rich members like Vincent Astor and the late William Gillette, the actor, who built little lines on their own land. Enthusiasm is their hallmark. Here is an item from one fan publication, offering pictures of the Western Pacific Railroad:

The Take Off! Wide open (running late), drivers spinning, hogger reefs her to the pin, down in the corner! . . . One of the most dynamic starts in steam I've ever lensed. Sand! L.I. L 3/4 complete, heavy train with desert background —clouds.

The steam lover appeared early on the scene. He insisted on a special preview ride, before regular service began, on the very first train in America. He went on camera excursions to Harpers Ferry before the Civil War. He reappeared in sizable numbers, in the middle twenties of this century, camera in hand and eager to be allowed, please, in the locomotive cab. Just as resolutely, at first, management ignored this unex-

pected offer of good will. Then, at last, it offered to show the fan around, but it failed abysmally to understand him. Come over here, said management, and see the streamliner. See our new diesel! But the fan wanted to ride a local and climb over a rusting steamer out behind the roundhouse. Management might as well have offered a date with a chorus girl to a man standing by the deathbed of his childhood sweetheart.

Perhaps the most outstanding example of what this organized enthusiasm can do is the story of the narrow-gauge Silverton passenger service of the Denver & Rio Grande Western Railroad, last survivor of a network of narrow-gauge lines hacked out of the Colorado mountains many decades ago—last, indeed, of all narrow-gauge passenger lines in America. A few years ago, it had dwindled to a twice-weekly mixed train, with a single passenger car, and application was made for its abandonment. Then the steam admirers took notice and moved in, until now, throughout the summer tourist months, the astonished railroad runs a train every day, with all its ten surviving cars packed solid. Not the least of the lures is that the power at the head end is honest old-fashioned steam. As in a horse opera, the rescue came in the nick of time, for the company had been gradually getting rid of its steamers by destroying them in head-on collisions staged for the movies.

From the steam fancier's standpoint, there is one more heartening piece of news, the situation at Lionel Lines, one of the healthiest corporations in the railroad business. Lionel, which manufactures model trains, has paid steady dividends since 1937 and the future looks only optimistic. As its president explains, he considers that his market comprises some 60 per cent of American males, young and old, and that demand for his product simply goes along with the birth rate. He has nowhere to go but up, and he plans to keep right on making steam engines.

A CONGRESSMAN'S PRAYER

Monday 4. December 1837
25 Congress 2. Session.

Almighty Father! Look in Mercy down:
Oh! grant me Virtue, to perform my part —
    The Patriots fervour, and the Statesmans art
In thought word, deed, preserve me from thy frown.

Direct me to the paths of bright Renown —
    Guide my frail bark, by Truth's unerring chart.
    Inspire my Soul; and purify my heart;
And with Success, my stedfast purpose crown.

My Country's weal — be that my Polar Star —
    Justice — thou Rock of Ages' is thy Law —
And when thy Summons calls me to thy bar
    Be this my plea, thy gracious smile to draw —
That all my ways to Justice were inclin'd
And all my aims — the Blessing of mankind.

J Q. Adams

This poem was not written for publication or to impress the constituents of the author, nor are these empty phrases. The gentleman from the Plymouth District of Massachusetts belonged to no party and meant every word he said. Placing duty before self, national interests before local, and justice before all, he served in the House through the long years between 1831 and 1848, when, at eighty, he died in honor at his post. No ordinary legislator, he had already been minister to Russia and the Court of St. James, professor of rhetoric and oratory at Harvard, secretary of state, and President of the United States. Who knows whether Congress will see the like again of such a poem or such a man as John Quincy Adams?

FOR THE USE OF THIS MANUSCRIPT WE ARE INDEBTED TO THE COLLECTION OF MR. AND MRS. DAN FERGUSON, BRIDWELL LIBRARY, SOUTHERN METHODIST UNIVERSITY.